AN ENCOURAGING THOUGHT

The **Christian Worldview** in the
Writings of J. R. R. Tolkien

DONALD T. WILLIAMS

AN ENCOURAGING THOUGHT

The Christian Worldview in the Writings of J. R. R. Tolkien

Donald T. Williams

Christian Publishing House

Cambridge, Ohio

Christian Publishing House

Professional Christian Publishing of the Good News

AN ENCOURAGING THOUGHT: The Christian Worldview in the Writings of J. R. R. Tolkien by Donald T. Williams

ISBN-13: 978-1-945757-79-2

ISBN-10: 1-945757-79-5

The West Of
Middle Earth
At The End Of
The Third Age

Table of Contents

Acknowledgements

A version of chapter two originally appeared as "An Encouraging Book: How Tolkien's Lord of the Rings Saved Me," *Touchstone: A Journal of Mere Christianity* 30:5 (Sept./Oct. 2017): 30-34. A version of part of the chapter on the LOTR movies was published as "The World of the Rings: Why Peter Jackson Was Unable to Film Tolkien's Moral Tale," *Touchstone: A Journal of Mere Christianity* 26:6 (Nov.-Dec. 2013): 14-16. A version of chapter five first appeared in *Inklings of Reality: Essays toward a Christian Philosophy of Letters* (Lynchburg: Lantern Hollow Press, 2012). The poems are from my book *Stars through the Clouds: The Collected Poetry of Donald T. Williams* (Lynchburg: Lantern Hollow Press, 2011). All that material is used here by permission.

PRELUDE the Undiscovered Country

The mind is poised; the fingers grip the pen.

    Ahead, the unexplored expanse of white

    Lies peaceful, undisturbed—invites you in.

    No one can tell what wondrous things you might

Encounter once the journey has begun:

    The hidden chambers of the human heart,

    That labyrinth that is fully known by none,

    Lie perilously open once you start.

Solar systems far beyond our ken;

    Dragons, wizards, elves, and warriors bold;

    The desperate lives of ordinary men;

    All the untold tales that must be told,

And any one might pick you for its Mage!

    The grand adventure of the empty page.

INTRODUCTION Joy and Rejuvenated Faith: Why the Inklings Matter

I first read *The Lord of the Rings* in the summer of 1968, the summer between my junior and senior years of high school. (I will never forget the chills running down my spine like the large, black, and angry summer thunderstorm that was rolling toward me across the Georgia Piedmont as I first encountered the Black Riders.) I checked the hardback volumes out of the library and devoured every page, including every last word of the appendices. My very next act after that was to buy the old Ballantine paperbacks (which cost a whopping ninety-five cents each at the time) and repeat the process.

I have read *The Hobbit* and *The Lord of the Rings* annually ever since (missing only a couple of years), and *The Silmarillion* several times as well. The only other work of prose fiction that comes close is *The Chronicles of Narnia*, which I read every couple of years. The only book to which I have devoted more time and effort as a reader is the Bible, which I also read cover to cover annually. My fellow Christians, even those who are also fellow fans of Tolkien and Lewis, might well ask why I devote *that* much time to them. Some of the answers will be found in this book.

I do not, of course, put Tolkien's and Lewis's books on the same level as Scripture. It is the inspired and infallible Word of God, and they are not.[1] But the first part of the answer to why I value their writings so highly is that they helped me greatly to find the path to fully appreciate what we have in the Bible.

---

[1] For some of the things that Lewis gets wrong (along with many more things he gets right), see my book *Deeper Magic: The Theology behind the Writings of C. S. Lewis* (Baltimore: Square Halo Books, 2016).

I was in that summer of 1968 going through a spiritual crisis that is familiar to a lot of people who grew up in Fundamentalist or conservative Evangelical churches. I had walked the aisle of a little country Baptist church at the advanced philosophical age of five to accept Christ as my Lord and Savior. That commitment was real and life-changing. But in a healthy discipling church it would have been the introduction to a lifetime of learning to follow John Donne's advice: "Employ then this noblest sense [sight] upon the noblest object. See God; see God in everything, and then thou needst not take off thine eye from . . . anything."[2] Unfortunately, we learned a lot of Bible and even some doctrine, but it did not seem to have anything much to do with how we saw the world beyond driving the necessary crises of getting saved, being baptized, joining the church, and rededicating your life. By the time I was in high school I had come to realize that not everybody saw things that way, and I was asking questions like "How do we know this is true?"

It was not so much the lack of answers that almost knocked my faith out of me; it was the attitude toward the questions. "If you were spiritual you wouldn't ask questions like that. You need to just read your Bible and pray more and have faith. You need to just believe." Now, on any other topic, if I asked you why I should believe something, and your answer was "You just need to believe it (for no reason I can give you)," I would immediately conclude that this would be a good belief to drop like the proverbial hot potato—indeed, I would chunk it as far away from me as I could. Why should this belief be different? Nobody seemed able to tell me.

Fortunately, Christianity is, in fact, true, which meant that Jesus was really present in my life, and He wasn't

---

[2] John Donne, "Sermon XXIII," in *Seventeenth-Century Prose and Poetry*, 2nd ed., ed. Alexander M. Witherspoon and Frank J. Warnke (NY: Harcourt, Brace, Jovanovich, 1982), 79.

about to let me get away from Him. So, I did not abandon the Faith, but for a while, I ceased being comfortable or at home in it. I had a nagging doubt I could not get rid of. I kept wanting to ask the church: "If you are so insecure in your beliefs that you are threatened by the questions of a half-educated kid, how could those beliefs possibly be true?"

In the providence of God, it was just then that the Tolkien craze of the Sixties hit my high-school campus. I was captivated by the Ring Trilogy, partly because it is such a great adventure story so well told, but also because I saw in it hints of biblical ideas that I was not used to encountering so strongly in "secular" literature. (I'll tell you what they are in chapter one.) And then somebody said, "If you like Tolkien you should check out his friend C. S. Lewis." My world was about to change forever.[3]

These men knew joy, not just as a passing emotion, but as the fountain of life. They gave me answers to my questions, some of which I will share in the chapters that follow. But just as important (maybe more so), they showed me that there was such a thing as a Christian mind by which such questions could *be* answered. A Christian mind was possible. It was not an oxymoron. And it took all of it you could muster to receive and understand and embrace the fullness of that joy. This did not just mean that there were good reasons to think that Christianity was true. It meant that, once you accept that truth, it reveals itself as the foundation of all truth and the key to understanding all of life and the whole world. It was the key that opened the door not just to escape from Hell but to a life full of meaning and of joy here and now, so much so that it was *worth* living for all of eternity.

---

[3] For a fuller account of my personal story, see my book *Inklings of Reality: Essays toward a Christian Philosophy of Letters*, 2nd ed. (Lynchburg: Lantern Hollow Press, 2012), 1-14.

I am not the only person on whom these two men have had this kind of influence. They not only helped preserve my Christian faith; they enriched and deepened it in more ways than I can count. Christians continue to appreciate their work and for good reason. Their popularity with and their influence on American Evangelicals show no sign of waning. That influence is a good thing that first deserves to be embraced and celebrated. Then it deserves nuanced appreciation and critical analysis. So, what can we learn from Tolkien about Christian truth and how it relates to the world? (See *Deeper Magic* for how I answer that question about Lewis.) What can we learn about what we believe, why we believe it, and so what if we believe it? Where is Tolkien not just a reliable but also an insightful guide to Christian truth and its implications? In what ways do Peter Jackson's film versions of Tolkien's books depart from that vision? Why do they depart from it? What does it all have to do with the way we see and live in the real world? Those are the sorts of questions we will begin to answer in the following pages.

In *Deeper Magic* I give a more advanced analysis of Lewis's *theology* from the total body of his work.[4] Lewis's more detailed approach to explaining the Christian faith makes such an analysis possible. Our aims here are more modest: an introduction to the Christian *worldview* in Tolkien, limited to his Middle Earth saga and a few of his other writings such as the essay "On Faerie Stories." I am going to assume, by the way, that you have already read *The Hobbit* and *The Lord of the Rings*. (Just seeing the movies doesn't count.) If you have not, what are you waiting for? Put this book down right now and go do so!

---

[4] On both men, see also my earlier book *Mere Humanity: G. K. Chesterton, C. S. Lewis, and J. R. R. Tolkien on the Human Condition* (Nashville: Broadman & Holman, 2006).

When you have, you will want to talk to someone about it. I'll still be here when you get back.

At one point in *The Lord of the Rings*, Gandalf tells Frodo that Bilbo was meant to find the Ring, and that this may be an encouraging thought. Why is that thought encouraging?

Let's find out!

INTERLUDE the Minstrel

The minstrel struck his golden harp;
The music sounded strong and clear,
Like edges keen and arrows sharp
    In hands of warriors bold.
Like rivers swift and mountains sheer,
Like the North wind blowing cold,
It stirred the very blood to hear
    Him strike his harp of gold.

And then the bard began to sing:
If all alone his melody
Could build so bright and shimmering
    A vision in the heart,
What charms of might and mystery
The spoken spell, the subtle art,
The wisdom and the wizardry
    Of wordcraft could impart!

So deep was the enchantment laid,
So masterful his minstrelsy,
So strong the music that he made,
    The story that he told,
That all the gathered chivalry
Would hearken 'til the night was old,
Entranced and still, whenever he
    Took up his harp of gold.

CHAPTER 1 "An Encouraging Thought": The Christian Vision of Middle Earth

I picked up *The Fellowship of the Ring* in the summer of 1968 out of idle curiosity over what all the "Frodo lives!" buttons and bumper stickers that had started showing up around Lakeshore High School in College Park, Georgia, were all about. I had no idea that Tolkien was a Christian. I was even a wee bit suspicious, thinking "Frodo lives" might be a blasphemous parody of Christian claims about the Resurrection of Jesus. (If it was, that was the fault of the fans, not of Tolkien himself.) I was not prepared to get swept off my feet in a manner that far outstripped my reaction to any other work of fiction I had ever read. But I did. Oh, boy, I surely did! And I remain fully swept to this day.

What was it that pulled me in? Was it the incarnational evocation of a world with its own unique, strong, quaint, and delicious flavor? Was it the simple beauty of the language and the absolute mastery of every style from the homely to the heroic, the vulgar to the valedictorian, according to the nature of the speaker? Was it characters like Gandalf and the Elves that you would give anything to meet in real life? Was it the grand adventure of a Quest with so much at stake? For me as for all of Tolkien's fans, it was doubtless the magic combination of all those things. I could not finish the three volumes quickly enough, and when I did, I could not stand the thought that it was over—so I started back through them again, more slowly, savoring every syllable—including every word of the appendices.

I had no idea that Tolkien was a Christian or that he would mark the turning point that would reverse my slide toward doubt and set me on the road to being not just a Christian but a Christian thinker and apologist. I just loved the story. But sometime in that second reading, the idea began slowly forming in my mind that, if a Christian ever did come alive to the mystery of life, the beauty and pathos of the world, and the power of words, this might be the way he would write. "Nah," I thought, "Not possible. No way that could ever happen." It was contrary to all my experience that there could be any such thing. But the thought would not go away. Where was it coming from?

I could not have articulated it then in the way I am about to do now, but there were five emphases or motifs in *The Lord of the Rings* that I was not used to seeing in quite the same way in "secular" literature—at least, not altogether in combination. (Of course, it is not at all accurate to classify *The Lord of the Rings* as "secular"—but I did not know that then.) They were biblical themes even in isolation, and much more powerfully so when taken together. They added up to a way of seeing the world that made it come alive and filled it with meaning. They would eventually form a lens through which I could come to see *this* world, not just the world of Tolkien's fiction, as one accurately described by biblical truth. What were they?

- ભ First, the way **Darkness and Light** interact symbolically in the story;

- ભ Second, the way what I will call **"the Strength of Weakness"** advances the plot to the point that you can't help but hear echoes of the biblical statement "Not by might, not by power, but by my Spirit, says the Lord" (Zech. 4:6) ringing through the story;

- ભ Third, the role of **Sacrifice** in the victories that are achieved;

- ભ Fourth, the hints of **Providence**, of a guiding Purpose behind supposedly chance events;

18

SR Finally, the presence of what I am tempted to call **Christ Figures** (though I will resist that temptation).

Together they add up to a story that resonates powerfully with Christian doctrine and with a biblical view of life and the world. Let's unpack them one at a time.

Darkness and Light

Darkness and light is a prominent theme in Scripture, as indeed it is in world literature in general. Darkness and light make natural symbols for ignorance and insight because you can see in the light and are relatively blind in the dark. They make natural symbols for good and evil because good has no fear of discovery while evil thrives under cover of darkness. So in Scripture, God is the one who created light and called it good (Gen. 1:3-4). God is Himself light, and in Him, there is no darkness at all (1 John1:5). He is the Father of Lights in whom is no variation or shifting shadow (James 1:17). Meanwhile, men love darkness rather than light because their deeds are evil (John 3:19) and salvation is described as being called out of darkness into light (1 Peter 2:9).

So, in *The Lord of the Rings*, Sauron is the *Dark* Lord who lives in Mordor, where the *shadows* lie. His most powerful servants are the *Black* Riders. (This is not a racial slur because the Nazgul are also referred to as *pale*; rather, it participates in the symbolism of darkness and light.) Arrayed against the forces of darkness is Gandalf, the *White* Rider, who is described as a servant of the *Secret Fire* and is even on a trivial level famous for his fireworks. One of the most powerful signs of encouragement and strength for those on the side of good is the *starlight* of Earendil which wells from the Phial of Galadriel (the *White* Lady of Loth Lorien).

Because darkness and light are natural and therefore universal symbols, their mere presence or even prominence in Tolkien's work is not necessarily evidence of specifically Christian content. A world in which good and evil are powerful, contrasting realities and not just arbitrary choices from the palette of cultural relativism is consistent with Christian teaching but does not necessarily specifically reflect it. But in *The Lord of the Rings*, there are telltale signs that the meaning of light to the good characters is tinged with explicitly Christian hope.

Sam Gamgee is a particular focus of this connection. Light has a way of finding him in his darkest moments to give him hope and strength to carry on. He fights off despair in the orc tower when all seems lost by singing this song:

> Though here at journey's end I lie
>> In darkness buried deep,
> Beyond all towers strong and high,
>> Beyond all mountains steep;
>
> Above all shadows rides the sun
>> And stars forever dwell.
> I will not say the day is done
>> Or bid the stars farewell.[5]

Later, Sam is reminded that Sauron's attempt to blot out the light with his darkness can never fully and finally succeed. There, looking up out of the desolation of Mordor,

> Sam saw a star twinkle for a while. The beauty of it smote his heart, as he looked up out

---

[5] Tolkien, *Return of the King*, 204-5.

of the forsaken land, and hope returned to him. For like a shaft clear and cold, the thought pierced him that in the end the Shadow was only a small and passing thing; there was light and high beauty forever beyond its reach.6

This is not then just a story of good versus evil. It is a story in which good and evil are opposed, but they are not equal. They are not just the light and dark "sides" of the same Force, as in the Star Wars universe. The Shadow which oppresses us and seems invincible is in the larger scheme only a small and passing thing. Final victory is forever beyond its reach, just as the clouds billowing from Mount Doom could never rise above the atmosphere to really put out a star in the heavens. That star and its light will remain when the wind has blown all of Sauron's gloom away. The star wins! Symbolically, good wins. No wonder Sam feels encouraged.

How can this be so? In a naturalistic universe, such a claim would be meaningless because good and evil are only subjective human perspectives and no finite human being can ever have the final word about anything. In a universe that was "spiritual" but not theistic (i.e., created by an infinite and personal God)—that is, in a pantheistic world like the world of Star Wars, the claim would be false. Neither good nor evil by definition can be ultimate there because both are merely aspects of the One reality that is all-encompassing. Therefore, their opposition is itself unavoidably eternal, unending. The light side might dominate for a while, but that is the most you can hope for. There can be no absolute victory ever because only a Sith deals in absolutes.

Note, by the way, the illogic of Obi Wan's statement to Anakin: "Only a Sith deals in absolutes." It is an absolute statement! The word "only" does not allow for any

---

6 Tolkien, *Return of the King*, 220.

21

exceptions to it. Therefore, as he has just dealt in an absolute himself, we must conclude that, based on his own definition, Obi Wan must be a Sith lord. But then what are he and Anakin fighting about? The entire Star Wars universe falls apart at that moment. And that cognitive collapse tells us that the pantheism that lies behind it cannot be true of the real world. Why not? It leads to a contradiction. Philosophers would say it is "self-referentially absurd." Any world in which the law of non-contradiction was not absolutely valid would unworld itself. It would tear itself apart. It could not be a *world*. Well, we find no such illogic in Middle Earth. Despite my love for the original Star Wars trilogy, I have to admit that it does not have the solid philosophical grounding that Tolkien's world does. And what is that grounding?

Only in a theistic universe, a universe created by an eternal, omnipotent, omniscient, and sovereign God, can the thought that comes to Sam be meaningful and true. In this world, goodness is not arbitrary but is rooted in the character of the creator God. Evil arises from the abuse of the free will God has granted his higher creatures and is tolerated for a while as the price of their significance. But it is derivative, not original, and thus doomed to eventual defeat because God as the Creator of all is the greatest Power that is or can be. He is sovereign; He retains ultimate control of the final outcome. Thus the ultimate triumph of good is guaranteed by the very nature of the world as created and its relationship to its Creator.

Now, most of the analysis in those last three paragraphs is only implied in *The Lord of the Rings*, not stated. And I was not philosophically sophisticated enough in 1968 to see all of those implications or to realize that only in a world created by a God very like the God of the Bible could such things be true.[7] But I instinctively

---

[7] Often they are treated as true in stories not written by people who believe in the Judeo-Christian Scripture or its God. Such writers

realized that in Middle Earth I was in a world in which hope could be more than wishful thinking, and it reminded me of the world of the Bible. That reminding was not an accident. The other four motifs that coordinate with it will confirm it.

Not By Might

Middle Earth has some impressively powerful heroes. Elrond has lore and knowledge that go back to the Elder Days. Faramir (in the books, not the movies[8]) has integrity and strength of character that is an inspiration. Legolas can shoot the eye out of a sparrow at a hundred yards with his bow, and as for Gimli's ax—well, I would not want to be anywhere nearby when he swings it. It would be hard to imagine a greater warrior or leader of men than Aragorn. Treebeard can crush stone into dust once he is aroused. And Gandalf, legendary for pyrotechnics and honored for wisdom, has an inner power that we never get to see fully uncloaked.

Now, the really curious thing is this: These heroes are exemplary, impressive, and inspiring, and they all have important roles to play. But none of them and none of their abilities (except perhaps Gandalf's wisdom) is the key to victory. No, this darkest of hours is the time when unforeseen by anyone but Gandalf, the little people, the hobbits, the Halflings of the Shire, arise to trouble the counsels of the Great. They are not just physically small. They are quiet and keep to themselves, and their little territory has zero impact on the nations and peoples

---

want good to win, they think it should, and they feel they will have a better story if it does. They have not thought these ideas through, though, and hence do not realize that they are cheating. Ultimately, only Christians can honestly believe in a happy ending.

[8] Unless otherwise stated, *all* of my references are to the books, not the movies.

around them. Most people don't even know they are there. Yet one of them finds the Ring, and another bears it. What is going on here? Let Elrond explain:

> The road must be trod, but it will be very hard. And neither strength nor wisdom will carry us far upon it. This quest may be attempted by the weak with as much hope as the strong. Yet it is oft the course of deeds that move the wheels of the world: small hands must do them because they must, while the eyes of the great are elsewhere.[9]

And so, it plays out. Frodo and Sam go alone under the very shadows of Mordor to destroy the Ring. Separated from the mighty Heroes who had been sent to guide and protect them, guided by Gollum, full of treachery, they somehow find a way. The hobbits have a kind of inner strength of their own, but even that is not what finally enables their success (though it does contribute to getting them to where they need to be to have that success). The last part of their journey seems to be nothing but failure. Frodo fails to reclaim Gollum from evil, Sam fails to protect Frodo from Gollum, Frodo fails to resist the temptation of the Ring and finally to secure it from Gollum, and even Gollum, who finally succeeds in his desperate quest to recover the Ring, cannot succeed in keeping it. Yet somehow out of all this failure—indeed, precisely as a result of it—victory is won. And the motif is woven deeper into the fabric of Middle Earth even than that. Even the Great and the Wise partake of it. We are to seek for the sword that was broken and remember that all that is gold does not glitter. It is the despised and forgotten Ranger who becomes the King of Men. Other stories, even without a biblical foundation, portray the

---

[9] Tolkien, *The Fellowship of the Ring*, 323.

conflict of good and evil. But hardly any other story resolves that conflict like this.

The only story I can think of that comes close is, once again, the biblical Story. God's propensity to create greatness out of human weakness and victory out of human defeat becomes apparent in the Old Testament and grows only to greater clarity as we move to the New. God chooses a wandering Aramaean couple who are unable to conceive a child and promises to make this barren family into a great nation which will bless every people on earth. That nation becomes a nation of slaves that wins its freedom not through the prowess of its own rebellion but through a series of plagues that come out of the blue. It has great heroes like Joshua and David, but their victories typically come in battles they never should have won so that it is obvious that the warrior who really saved them was Yahweh. This motif is implicit in the narrative and made explicit by prophecy: "The Lord did not set His love on you nor choose you because you were more in number than any of the peoples, for you were the fewest of all peoples, but because the Lord loved you and kept the oath which He swore to your forefathers" (Deut. 7:7, cf. 8:17-18, 9:4f, etc.).

Then in the New Testament, the same pattern continues and is brought to fruition. Jesus is born to a peasant couple who can't find a motel, and his first cradle is a feeding trough. He is trained as a tradesman, not a rabbi, and most of his disciples are uneducated fishermen. He shows Himself Master of the winds and the waves and even of death, but it is not those miracles that change the world. Rejected by the religious establishment and deserted by most of his followers, he is executed as a criminal and buried in a borrowed tomb. Nobody could find a shred of hope for the world in such a story—yet this is how sins are forgiven, and death defeated, and the world turned upside down. And the motif continues in

25

the Church that Jesus founded: Not many great or wise (as the world sees them) are called, but rather the weak and foolish are called to shame the wise and the strong. Why? So that no one can boast (1 Cor. 1:27-9).

It is important to see the point the Bible draws from this motif, for it is the same point conveyed by its appearance in Middle Earth. It is not that wisdom, intelligence, strength, or skill, much less integrity and benevolence, are to be despised or not appreciated. In the Bible, we are to love the Lord our God with all our heart, soul, *and mind* (Matt. 22:37). In the Old Testament, Israel was to worship God with the sacrifice of an *unblemished* male of the flock (Exodus 12:5, etc.). George Herbert summarizes this theme perfectly: "My God must have my best, even all I had."[10] We give God our best, physically, mentally, and morally, because He deserves no less—not because we think our best is worthy of Him or adequate to achieve His purposes. We give Him our best efforts because He is worthy, but we do not trust in them but in Him. So in the saga of Middle Earth, victory is not won without the best sacrificial efforts of the Great and the Wise, nor could it have been. But it could not have been won *by* those efforts either. Something much deeper had to be at work, as we shall see.

This Scriptural motif of the ironic strength of weakness (when it is used by God) is summed up in the words "Not by might, not by power, but by my Spirit, says the Lord" (Zech. 4:6). And it is present so strongly in *The Lord of the Rings* that even as a high-school student giving the book my second reading in 1968, I had to wonder whether that could possibly be so by accident. As I was to discover, it was not.

---

[10] George Herbert, "The Forerunners," Witherspoon and Warnke, 858.

26

Sacrifice

In the War of the Ring, then, victory is won, not in spite of, but *through* what at least looks like weakness and failure. But there is yet another very biblical motif that comes along with the strength of weakness and is inextricably intertwined with it: the theme of sacrifice.

In the Christian faith, what is it that turns the apparent defeat and failure of the crucifixion into victory? Certainly, part of the answer is that the crucifixion was the *sacrifice* of Christ for the sins of His people. His death paid the penalty of death that we owed for our sins. He paid it on our behalf so that we could be set free from it. Christ died for us, in our place. He died so that we could live. In theology, this is called "vicarious penal substitution." Substitution: Christ died in our place; vicarious: He does for us what we cannot do for ourselves; penal: He takes the punishment our sins deserved. Jesus came to "give his life a ransom for many" (Matt. 20:28). Because of who Jesus was—the eternal Son of God who became the Son of Man—His sacrificial death has this saving significance that turns defeat into victory and leads to His resurrection and eventually ours.

We cannot look for an exact parallel in the Ring Trilogy because there is no one with the status of Christ, the kind of status that could give his death (or any other sacrifice he might make) the same kind of impact. But the story is full of meaningful acts that become meaningful and make a difference precisely because they are sacrificial. Pippin casts away his Elven brooch on the chance it would give a sign to Aragorn. "It was a wrench to let it go," Pippin says, "but what else could I do?" "Nothing else," Aragorn replies. "One who cannot cast away a treasure at need is in fetters. You did rightly."[11] There are more

---

[11] Tolkien, *The Two Towers*, 199.

profound sacrifices. Arwen gives up her immortality for a life with Aragorn, and thus her spot on the ship to Valinor to Frodo.[12] And Frodo wants to save the Shire and pays a terrible price to do so. "No taste of food, no feel of water, no sound of wind, no memory of tree or grass or flower, no image of moon or star are left to me. I am naked in the dark, Sam, and there is no veil between me and the wheel of fire."[13] The full nature of his sacrifice only becomes clear to him after the fact, when he realizes that a peaceful retirement in the Shire is not possible for him. "I have been too deeply hurt, Sam. I tried to save the Shire, and it has been saved, but not for me. It must often be so, Sam, when things are in danger. Someone has to give them up, lose them, so that others may keep them."[14]

It is not an atonement—for that we would need Christ (or Aslan). But it is vicarious suffering which becomes the key to deliverance for others, given freely and nobly. As such it is one more element that resonates strongly with the biblical story and thus strengthens the resonance of the other elements we have been seeing.

Providence

One of the places where the influence of the biblical worldview on *The Lord of the Rings* is most pervasive is in the many hints that Middle Earth is governed by a personal Providence that gives purpose and meaning to what happens. In *The Hobbit*, Bilbo is blessed with an unusual supply of personal "good luck" which helps him out of various scrapes in his adventures. The first clear hint that there is more to it than that appears on the very last page. Bilbo and Gandalf are reminiscing about their adventures

---

[12] Tolkien, *The Return of the King*, 282.

[13] Tolkien, *The Return of the King*, 238.

[14] Tolkien, *The Return of the King*, 345.

and Bilbo marvels that all the prophecies in the old songs came true after all.

> "Of course," said Gandalf, "and why should not they prove true? Surely you don't disbelieve the prophecies because you had a hand in bringing them about yourself? You don't really suppose, do you, that all your adventures and escapes were managed by mere luck, just for your sole benefit? You are a very find person, Mr. Baggins, and I am very fond of you, but you are only quite a little fellow in a wide world after all!"

"Thank goodness!" said Bilbo laughing, and handed him the tobacco-jar.[15]

Gandalf's cryptic comment raises some intriguing questions. If Bilbo's adventures and escapes were not managed by mere luck, what were they managed by? If they were not managed for his sole benefit, what were they managed for? And can a "what" really "manage" anything? Don't we really need a "who" for that?

The Hobbit raises such questions, and *The Lord of the Rings* does not exactly answer them—but it does provide further hints and clues that make the questions more insistent. In *The Hobbit*, Bilbo's luck is usually simply mentioned without comment, right up to that last conversation about it with Gandalf. In the sequel, the words *luck* and *chance* appear often, but almost never without a comment by either a character or the narrator: "If luck/chance you call it." This persistently raises the question whether it should be called something else. All this hinting comes into a bit more focus in Bag End when Gandalf is bringing Frodo up to date on the history of the Ring. "I can put it no plainer than by saying that Bilbo was

---

[15] Tolkien, *The Hobbit*, 303.

meant to find the Ring, and *not* by its maker. . . . And that may be an encouraging thought."[16]

Again, Tolkien does not give us the answer, but he encourages us—yea, sets us up—to ask a very pertinent question. I was I must confess a bit puzzled by this passage as an upcoming high-school senior. "What is encouraging about this thought?" I wanted to know. "Why is it encouraging? What makes it encouraging?" I only slowly began to understand the answer, but from the beginning, I was asking the right question, the question I am convinced Tolkien wanted his readers to ask. I would begin to see the answers to it slowly coming into focus with each successive reading.[17]

Meaning is an inherently and inescapably personal category. In order for there to be meaning, there has to be someone some person, to *mean* the meaning. The twenty-six letters of the English alphabet have no particular meaning by themselves. But what if I deliberately arrange them into the form of this paragraph? Then there is a message for them to convey, a message that resulted from my meaningful act. I did it so that you would get the meaning that meaning comes from personal action. With that personal action, there is a meaning here for you to get (or to miss). Without it, there would be no meaning to letters you just found lying around at all, except one that you just arbitrarily made up. There is a real *meaning* here because I *meant* there to be—that is, I intended or purposed to communicate it.

In just the same way, in order for there to be a purpose, there has to be someone to intend the purpose.

---

[16] Tolkien, *The Fellowship of The Ring*, 81.

[17] See Devin Brown, *The Christian World of* The Hobbit (Nashville: Abingdon, 2012), chapter II, "'Luck of an Unusual Kind': Providence in *The Hobbit*," for an excellent survey of relevant passages in both *The Hobbit* and *The Lord of the Rings*.

(You see that meaning and purpose or intent are inextricably intertwined.) Things that don't have a person behind them don't happen for a reason; they just happen because they happen to happen. The rock that falls off the cliff above you and hits you in the head wasn't trying to hurt you, and neither was the cliff. The rock your enemy threw at you is a different matter altogether. Just as there is no meaning, so also there is no purpose without a person behind it. There can't be.

Alright, then: If Bilbo was meant to find the Ring, there had to be someone to mean that he would find it, someone working behind the scenes to ensure he would find it; it wasn't just an accident. And if this person was not Sauron, it had to be someone greater than Sauron, someone, capable of causing things to happen that Sauron could not control or even anticipate. And if that is true, then we may be encouraged by the thought indeed, for it means that ultimate victory may not depend just on Frodo's strength or Gandalf's schemes.

If it is just Frodo or even all the Nine Walkers pitted against Sauron, they don't have a fighting chance. That there is no hope of a final military victory for the West, that no such victory against the forces amassed against them is possible, is emphasized over and over again. For two hobbits of the Shire, guided in the end only by the treacherous Gollum, ever to make it alive across the plains of Mordor and reach the Chamber of Fire, is equally impossible. If that plan was all Gandalf and Elrond had, if they had no insight or vision beyond that, then their hope was a fool's hope indeed, as Gandalf is often reminded. But if there is some greater force at work—and if Gandalf has some real insight into that reality, some real basis for his faith in it—well, that changes everything. Then it is not just an accident that in both *The Hobbit* and its sequel people keep coming by "the only road that was any good,"[18] even when it looked like a pure disaster. And if we really mean the word *meant*, then the explanation for those outcomes cannot just be an impersonal force. Only persons have purposes. (The Star Wars universe also falls apart every time some character speaks of "the will of the Force.") Only persons can mean, or purpose, or will things. Therefore, this person working behind the scenes in Frodo's life is one we are tempted to think of as a Person. Could it be God?

From *The Lord of the Rings* alone, we cannot tell who this person is, or even if he is a real person and not just a confused metaphor. But we are definitely asked to start wondering about such things. I certainly was in the late Sixties. And confirmation of the answer was coming.

Christ Figures?

The last clue that got my attention in the summer of 1968 was a series of characters that reminded me of Jesus in ways that seemed too specific to be accidental. But before I talk about them, let me address the question mark in the heading above. To call anyone in *The Lord of the Rings* a "Christ figure" is to say too much. Tolkien was too wise to ask any of his characters to carry such a heavy load. There is no one who functions like Aslan does in C. S. Lewis's Narnia stories, and to try to fit any character into such a mold is to strain credibility. Nevertheless, there are indeed characters that do hint at certain aspects of Christ's person or His work so that these hints resonate with the other biblical themes we have already seen.

It is traditional in theology to speak of Christ as having three "offices," three roles that He plays in the achievement of our salvation and the management of history: He is Prophet, Priest, and King.

---

[18] Tolkien, *The Hobbit*, 189.

32

As Prophet, Christ reveals God the Father to the world. He is the Word who was with God and was God in the beginning, the Light that, coming into the darkness of this world, enlightens every man; No one has seen God at any time, but he only begotten God who is in the bosom of the Father has declared Him (John 1:1-18). In these last days God has spoken to us in His Son, who is the radiance of His glory and the exact representation of His nature (Heb. 1:2-3). By what He said and by what He did, especially in His sacrificial death and triumphant resurrection, Jesus shows us who God is and what He is like: absolutely just and demanding the death penalty for sin, but so loving that He takes that penalty on Himself.

As Priest, Christ made atonement for the sins of His people. This atonement was the fulfillment of the Old-Testament sacrificial system administered by the Aaronic high priest, so Christ as Priest is an apt metaphor for this crucial aspect of His work. (Actually, He transcended the Aaronic prefiguring so radically in fulfilling it that He is given a new order of priesthood, that of Melchizedek.) In the Old-Testament preparation for Christ's coming, a perfect victim from the flock was sacrificed as a sin offering so that the people could be forgiven. The Priesthood of Christ then refers to His suffering for us. He gave up His prerogatives as the Son of God and the glories of Heaven and even His life for our sake. He gave these things up for a time so that we could keep them forever.

The Kingship of Christ refers of course to His reigning as Lord over all of creation. Because He humbled Himself even to death on a cross, "Therefore God also highly exalted Him and bestowed upon Him the name that is above every name, so that at the name of Jesus every knee should bow . . . and every tongue confess that Jesus Christ is Lord to the glory of God the Father" (Phil. 2:9-11). Jesus is Lord of Lords and King of Kings, but the full exercise of that kingship, the full coming of that kingdom, is something we have to wait for. His kingdom is one that has to be restored—when the King returns.

Tolkien has characters who remind you of these three offices of Christ, and of Christ's way of fulfilling them, but he wisely keeps them separate, so that no single person is trying to combine them all in one. That way, each character can stay believable in his own role, and the story can be full of symbolic Christian significance without being pulled in the direction of an allegory where the theological "lessons" threaten to take over and become too obvious, to the detriment of the story as a story.

Gandalf is the Prophet. He is an unerring source of not just wisdom but also vision. He is the one who sees what needs to be done and can find people willing to do it. He gives people the faith to look beyond the needs of the moment to the needs of Middle Earth. But while his primary role is as a prophet, he pursues it in ways that remind you of Christ in that role and others as well. He dies and returns from death. He is a light shining in the darkness. He conceals great power and glory that on occasion shine forth (as Christ's did on the Mount of Transfiguration). And he is a man of sorrows and acquainted with grief, a bearer of great burdens, who nonetheless is a fountain of joy. "In the wizard's face, Pippin saw at first only lines of care and sorrow, though as he looked more intently, he perceived that under all there was a great joy, a fountain of mirth enough to set a kingdom laughing were it to gush forth."[19]

Frodo, and in a lesser way Sam, plays the role of the Priest. The parallels are not *too* close: He does not make atonement for sin, and he does not, like Gandalf, die and come back to life. But Frodo makes great sacrifices for the sake of The Shire and voluntarily takes on great suffering so that others will not have to. The cost of bearing the

---

[19] Tolkien, *The Return of the King*, 33.

34

Ring is heavy. "No taste of food or water, no memory of tree or grass or flower, no image of moon or star is left to me. I am naked in the dark, Sam, and there is no veil between me and the wheel of fire."[20] He saves The Shire but is too deeply wounded to enjoy the fruits of his victory. Someone has to lose things, he tells Sam so that others can keep them.[21] Frodo reminds us of Christ in the way he freely chooses to suffer for others.

Finally, Aragorn is the King. He is the rightful king, the heir of Isildur, but we spend most of the trilogy *waiting* for his kingdom to come. When it finally does, it ushers in a new age of peace for Middle Earth. I suppose any good king is a picture of the King of Kings merely by virtue of his office, but Tolkien goes out of his way to let us know that in Aragorn the resemblance runs deep. "Thus spake Ioreth, wise woman of Gondor: *The hands of the king are the hands of a healer, and so shall the rightful king be known.*"[22]

Gandalf; Frodo; Aragorn: None of these characters is exactly a Christ figure in the full sense of that phrase, though perhaps cumulatively they add up to one. It is better that they are not. But it is no accident, as I would eventually discover, that Tolkien's heroes remind us of the true Hero of the larger Story, the Gospel. They do so because of the profound ways in which their author had absorbed a higher ideal of heroism from the biblical text.

Conclusion

To a discerning eye, then, the content of Christian doctrine is powerfully present in *The Hobbit* and *The Lord of the Rings*, not just in statements made by various characters or the narrator, but in the very structure of the

---

[20] Tolkien, *The Return of the King*, 238.

[21] Tolkien, *The Return of the King*, 345.

[22] Tolkien, *The Return of the King*, 152.

plot. Darkness and light are used as symbols, and characters apply those symbols to themselves, in ways that are not only consistent with Christian teaching but are in fact *fully* consistent with nothing else. And the plot moves toward its resolution by means of the strength of weakness, enabled by a purposeful Providence through sacrifice, to produce a *eucatastrophe*, a happy ending, reminiscent of the Gospel itself. The heroes of the story remind us of the greatest Hero in ways that are not incidental, but fundamental, to who they are and who He is.

This is all done subtly enough that it is possible to miss it, though the better readers know their Bible and some Christian teaching the more likely they will be to see it. Shippey says it well: "*The Lord of the Rings*, then, contains within it hints of the Christian message, but refuses just to repeat it."[23] As a young reader not even looking for such things, I saw the hints. Those hints were soon to become clear signs planted solidly in the bedrock of Middle Earth. But that is the story of another chapter.

---

[23] Shippey, Tom. *J. R. R. Tolkien: Author of the Century* (Boston: Houghton Mifflin, 2000), 210.

INTERLUDE A Glimmer of Hope

When Bilbo Baggins ran off down the road
    Without a hat or pocket handkerchief
    Or even proper time to say, "Good bye,"
Did Smaug, asleep in his usurped abode,
    Dream of Burglars stealing from the Thief?
    Did Sauron shudder without knowing why?

The hobbit, Gandalf later said, was *meant*
    To find the Ring: a thought to bring relief
    To Frodo's mind when it was asking, "Why?"
Iluvatar had left at least that glint
    For them to spy.

CHAPTER 2 "Eucatastrophe": Middle Earth and the Christian World View

In the summer of '68 the five themes we have just studied in chapter one, especially as they interacted with and played off of each other, were sufficient to make me seriously wonder whether Tolkien might, if such a thing were not impossible, be a Christian. But still, at that time, they were hints, nothing more. From the text of the novels alone, you could not prove—at least, I was not yet sophisticated enough to do so—that they were anything more than hints and suggestions, that they added up to a solid interpretation. Still, I did what you do when you find an author who moves you deeply. I proceeded to get ahold of every word he had published and ravenously devour them all.

In 1968, beyond *The Hobbit* and *The Lord of the Rings*, there wasn't very much. But there was a little collection called *The Tolkien Reader*, and it contained an essay entitled "On Fairie Stories." My world was about to change forever. In this chapter, we will document that change and see how it confirmed that my guesses were more than guesses because the hints were more than hints. More importantly, the way I learned that lesson will show us how Tolkien's work communicates not just certain Christian ideas but also a biblical *worldview*. We will also look at why that second step matters.

Confirmation

"On Faerie Stories" was an *apologia* for treating the Fairy Story as a serious art form and contained tantalizing suggestions about the composition of *The Lord of the Rings*. As such, it was interesting enough. Tolkien was explaining such stories as an example of his notion of sub-creation: Human beings are creative because they are created in the image of the Creator. At a climactic moment, he quoted from his own poem "Mythopoeia," written as part of an argument with his friend C. S. Lewis and summarizing the case Tolkien had made to the not yet converted Lewis on Addison's Walk in Oxford that led to Lewis's coming to Christ. I did not find that bit of backstory out until later, but it made plenty of sense when I did. Tolkien's words certainly had an impact on *my* unsuspecting mind! Suddenly and without warning, a full rank of Gandalf's fireworks went off inside my head.

Although now long estranged,

Man is not wholly lost nor wholly changed.

Dis-graced he may be, yet is not de-throned,

And keeps the rags of lordship once he owned:

Man, Sub-creator, the refracted Light

Through whom is splintered from a single White

To many hues, and endlessly combined

In living shapes that move from mind to mind. . . .

Used or misused, that right has not decayed:

We make still by the law in which we're made.[24]

My hands still shake with excitement when I read the note I scribbled into the margin that day: "I.e., Tolkien's theory is inherently Christian and assumes the *imago Dei* [image of God]." And as if he had known that such a revelation might seem too good to be true, he confirmed the poetry in plain prose only one page later: "We make . . . because we are made: and not only made, but made in the image and likeness of a Maker."[25] It is called

---

[24] Tolkien, "On Faerie Stories," 54; emphasis added.
[25] Tolkien, "On Faerie Stories," 55.

Tolkien's doctrine of "sub-creation." Then at the end of the essay, he speaks even more explicitly: The Gospel is a fairy story (with a supremely Happy Ending). "But this story has entered History and the primary world." In other words, "There is no tale ever told that men would rather find was true, and none which so many skeptical men have accepted as true on its own merits. . . . This story is supreme, and it is true."[26]

It was one of those rare moments of white-hot insight that illuminates the whole dark world like a lightning bolt at midnight, drives away the shadows, and etches the true shape of things in your consciousness forever. There was only one thing to do: I slammed the book shut and went for a walk to reorganize my entire mental landscape.

Tolkien was a Christian! He not only accepted very specific Christian doctrine, the creation of humanity in the image of God, as true; he based his entire literary theory on that truth. And he said, very publicly, that the Gospel was true and historical and of supreme importance and the grounds for hope in the best Happy Ending ever. Therefore, all the hints of Christian truth and meaning I had seen in the Trilogy must not be accidents or figments of my imagination after all, but flowed from their author's own deepest convictions about the world—*this* world, as well as his own, created one. Not that he had written the books as a kind of religious propaganda—they were too good a story as a story for that—but his biblical way of seeing the world had naturally found its way to expression in his greatest work. That such a thing could happen was to me good news only second to that of the Gospel itself.

Further confirmation was on its way. Not quite a decade later the long-awaited prequel to *The Lord of the Rings* came out. *The Silmarillion* is not a finished work. Edited by Tolkien's son from his father's notes, it is not as

---

26 Tolkien, "On Faerie Stories," 71-2.

well developed or as polished at the Ring trilogy and lacks the anchoring of the high and noble in a recognizably human world provided by the hobbits. It is not the masterpiece that the trilogy is, but those who love Middle Earth value it for its own sake and for the way it fleshes out the hints in the appendices. Nevertheless, it does contain "The Ainulindale," the creation story of Middle Earth. And that is one of the most beautiful and profound passages Tolkien ever wrote.

There was Iluvatar, the One, and the Ainur, the children of Iluvatar (roughly corresponding to the angels). Iluvatar sings to them a great theme of music and asks them to form it into a symphony, with each of them, according to his stature, contributing notes, and elaborations. But Melkor (the Satan figure) decides to make his own music, a harsh and braying sound not in harmony with the rest. Some of the Ainur join him, while others try to maintain the original melody. There is a great war in heaven between these two versions of the music until Iluvatar introduces a second and a third theme which takes up the notes of Melkor and dovetails them back into the work, overcoming the cacophony in a final resolution. Then while everyone is looking around wondering, "What just happened?" Iluvatar says,

> Mighty are the Ainur, and mightiest among them is Melkor; but that ye may know . . . that I am Iluvatar, those things that ye have sung, I will show them forth, that ye may see what ye have done. And thou, Melkor, shalt see that no theme may be played that hath not its uttermost source in me, nor can any alter the music in my despite. For he that attempteth this shall prove but mine instrument in the devising of things

more wonderful, which he himself hath not imagined.[27]

The music as thus shown forth then becomes the history of the world, and some of the Ainur (who become known as the Valar) enter into this new Middle Earth to guide that history in accordance with the music. Melkor thus becomes known as Morgoth, the great Enemy of the First Age of Middle Earth. Sauron, the super-villain of the Third Age, is a servant of Morgoth. And thus all the hints of *The Lord of the Rings* are revealed not as hints but as solid signposts. For now, we know that not only is Tolkien a believer in God, but Middle Earth is an explicitly theistic world. Now we know that darkness and light, the strength of dedicated weakness, sacrifice, providence, and Christlike heroes are not just accidental resemblances to Christian ideas but are foundational to the very existence and significance of Middle Earth. Now we know that the One who meant Bilbo to find the Ring is most definitely a Person with a name: Eru Iluvatar, the One. And now we know why that fact is an encouraging thought.

Tolkien and the Christian Worldview

The Nature of the Christian World View

I did not in the summer of 1968 know that there was such a thing as a worldview, nor that the Christian faith had one. (I would learn that phrase from Francis Schaeffer in the following year.) But reading *The Lord of the Rings* and the process of confirming my hunches about its meaning via the essay "On Fairie Stories" was what got me started in the process of acquiring a biblical worldview. For I realized that it was possible to think Christianly about the world. In other words, Christian doctrines were not

---

[27] Tolkien, *The Silmarillion*, 17.

just things—Creation, the Fall, the Birth, Death, Resurrection, and future Return of Christ—that we believed had happened in the past. They are also descriptions of the way the world is, of what reality is like. We live in the kind of world that would be created by that kind of God, the God who is a Trinity, the God who would enter into that world's history in the Person of His Son and redeem it through His own sacrificial death. We live in a world that is that kind of world, and that has had precisely that history. The Christian faith is not just a story we tell ourselves on Sunday to make us feel better; it is real truth about the world, historically, factually, and metaphysically. If it isn't, it is worthless.

To say that Christianity is a worldview is to say that it is not just a set of beliefs one happens to hold as part of one's religion, but it is a unified way of looking at the world in the light of those beliefs *held as true*. It takes their basic motifs, such as creation, fall, redemption, and restoration, not just as ideas we happen to believe in but as realities that are foundational to all other beliefs about the world that we might hold. Thus, Christian doctrine is not just a way of organizing our religious feelings; it is the key that fits the lock of the world around us. It is what lets us understand it in the light of its meaning, purpose, and destiny. It organizes and focuses all our responses (not just our emotions, though they are definitely not left out) to what we see and experience. It informs our understanding, energizes our wills, and directs our choices about every aspect of life, not just our religion, on every day of the week, not just on Sunday. Every fact we discover about the world is seen in the light of the fundamental conviction that the world is a purposefully created place made by a personal and infinite God who has made us in His image and communicated His existence to us in nature, in history, through the prophets and apostles (spokesmen who speak to us intelligibly about these truths), and ultimately through Christ, who is the Source, the Center, and the Key of all.

Christians see the same facts as the non-Christian, in other words, but because of this worldview we see them differently; we see them in a larger, indeed in a far richer, context. The typical non-Christian looks at arithmetic, for example, and says, "Two plus two make four. I've no idea why—it just seems to work. Whatever." The Christian who sees the same numbers through the lens of the biblical worldview can say, "Two plus two make four, and this is a glorious example of the beautiful rationality of the mind of God." Both of them balance their checkbooks, and they (hopefully) get the same sum, but for only one of them is getting that sum an act of worship. In Augustinian terms, both have *Scientia* (knowledge) of math, but only one has *Sapientia* (wisdom) about it. The fear of the Lord is the beginning of wisdom.

Same facts; different significance. For the Christian who has learned to think world-viewishly, this is not just a subjective emotional patina spread over the same facts; it is a more fully human response to those facts that is completely justified by seeing them more clearly, in the only context that makes it finally possible to make sense of them. It makes sense of them because it is the only context in which they can be seen as properly related to their Source.

The realization that Christianity is not just a religion but also a worldview does two things. First, it confirms our faith because we can see that looking at the world as if the Christian story is actually true is the key to better answers to the philosophical problems raised by life in this world than its rival belief systems can give.[28] Second, it

---

[28] If you are interested in exploring ways this is true, I recommend three books: Francis Schaeffer's *The God Who is There* (Downers Grove, IL: InterVarsity Press, 1968) and *He is There and He is Not Silent*

helps us understand the world we live in—not just our "religion" but the world itself. Just in this way, his belief in the Gospel helped Tolkien understand human nature as it is expressed in and inspired by fairy stories. How specifically does Tolkien help us to see these things?

These discoveries really began to hit me hard when, after devouring *The Lord of the Rings,* I read the essay "On Faerie Stories." For that essay made it evident that Tolkien didn't just believe the Gospel on Sunday. He treated it as true the rest of the week and *applied* it to the literary phenomenon he was studying as a scholar—and it produced tremendous insights. He read the same fairy stories as everybody else, but because he believed the Gospel and treated it as true, he saw things in them that others had missed. And then when he looked at them more closely in their linguistic, literary, and historical contexts, that vision of them was confirmed. (This is an important element. An interpretation is not true just because it resonates with Christian belief; it also has to fit the facts and be supported by the evidence!). And *that* confirmed the truth of the Gospel that had helped him see those things in the first place. Its truth was confirmed by its fruitfulness as a lens through which to see life.

This rootedness of Christian belief in a comprehensive and unified view of the world and of life was what had been missing from my early religious upbringing. Its absence was what left me open to doubts I could not resolve on my own. So it was tremendously important to me to discover that a brilliant linguist, writer, and thinker like Tolkien affirmed his faith in Christ. But it was even more important that he let me see him treating those beliefs as true outside of the church, applying them with confidence in what was not an overtly religious context— his literary scholarship. "You can *do* that?" I thought at the

(Wheaton, IL: Tyndale House, 1972), and my *Reflections from Plato's Cave* (Lynchburg: Lantern Hollow Press, 2012).

time. "*I* want to do that!" (I've been trying to do it ever since.) Pretty soon Tolkien's friend C. S. Lewis, whose Christianity was even more up-front and conspicuous in his writings, and then a little later Francis Schaeffer, would show me more about how it is done. But it was Bilbo, Frodo, Aragorn, and Gandalf who first showed me that it *could* be done. That changed everything.

The Content of the Christian World View

What exactly is this Christian worldview I keep talking about? A worldview relates everything it experiences back to a single fundamental starting point which becomes a reference point for answering the Big Questions. What does everything come from? The answer we give to that question becomes the key to how we answer the other ones that come after it. Who are we? Why are we here? What does it all mean? How do we know?

All right, then. A Christianity that understands itself doesn't just take the secular world science reveals and then add God to it as a big magical being who is hiding out there in it somewhere. It starts by asking, "What is the origin of all things?" Does an impersonal physical world just happen to exist for no reason, or was the world created on purpose by a personal and purposeful God? How you answer that question determines how you will see everything else.

How then do we answer it? What are the options available to us? And what are the implications of those choices? If everything just goes back to matter, energy, time, and chance—to the impersonal—then good and evil, right and wrong, are just names we attached arbitrarily to things we happened to like or not like. They have no ultimate meaning because they are inescapably *personal*, and the universe is ultimately *impersonal*. Thus there is no real place for them except as subjective viewpoints we cling to. They are not and cannot be truths about the real world. Meaning and purpose in such a world are just concepts we make up to distract ourselves from the reality that stuff just happens for no reason, and nobody has a right to tell us that we should have made them up differently.

O.K., that's one option. What is the alternative? What if the origin of all things is not an impersonal universe after all, but something Personal? If the world was created by a personal and purposeful God, then personal categories like right, wrong, good, evil, purpose, and meaning are back on the table again. And that is the only way they can be back on the table when they not just subjective feelings, but reflections of reality, of the way the world actually is because they are rooted in the very source of reality, which is Personal.

The secular (impersonal) way of looking at the world has become increasingly dominant over the last couple of generations. Why? Because too often even people who are Christians in their religious life *think* as if the secular worldview of naturalistic science—everything goes back to the impersonal interactions of atoms—is true. Their Christian faith is an outlier, an exotic plant trying to grow in the foreign intellectual soil of secularity because they have never been taught that it has anything to do with how they see the world. Their teachers have unthinkingly accepted the premise of modern culture that religion is purely an internal matter of the "heart."

You see, in the secular worldview, if something is personal, then the only place it can be real is inside of you—not outside of you in the "real" impersonal world that everybody else has to live in when they are not inside of themselves. That is why this generation is only able to think of ideas as true "for me" or "for you"—not as just plain true, period. Well, Christian faith cannot be less than an internal matter of the heart, but it must be more if it is to be credible even to those who hold it, much less to the other people they were sent to reach. It has to be true to the heart *and* the head to be believable as anything more than just a private fantasy.

Often, when such Christians' religious leaders do realize that their faith is contradicted by the secular worldview, they act as if it were contradicted by *science*— rather than by the *interpretation* of what science has learned about the world that is generated by the secular *worldview*, as opposed to the facts themselves. They can't tell them apart; they simply do not understand the difference. Thus their faith survives only by becoming isolated from (and irrelevant to) contemporary thought and culture. They do not understand that the exotic plant of faith can only survive and be healthy when it is rooted in its native soil of reality—a reality bigger than just what is true inside of you. That was precisely what I needed to understand in order to get past my own doubts back in 1968. And we can see that the claims of Christ are rooted in reality when we learn to think about faith on the level of worldview. And that is why I can say that I owe my preservation in the faith to reading *The Lord of the Rings*.

The Basis of the Christian World View

O.K., Christianity is more than just a religion; it is a worldview. And because that worldview starts with the God who in the beginning (like Iluvatar) created the heavens and the earth, it claims to have truth that is not just for internal emotional consumption but is true about those heavens and that earth, about the world. Well, is this Christian worldview just a nice theory, or is it really true? There are as many reasons to believe that the Christian faith is true as there are facts in the world that are rightly interpreted by its worldview! But let me give you just a brief overview of some of the more significant

48

ones. There are at least three good reasons not to look at the world the way the secular worldview does, and the biblical worldview is the only viable alternative to it on the market. (Other religions either don't really have a creator God, or if they do, he has not stuck his neck out in history so we can verify his claims the way the God of the Bible did when He sent his Son to be born in Bethlehem and die for our sins at the hands of the Roman Empire.)

First, nobody can actually live as if life is meaningless—as it must be if the origin of all things is impersonal matter. Many people have accepted that life must be meaningless on the basis of the secular worldview, but hardly any of them live consistently with that belief. People who believe life has no meaning or purpose and that objective truth is a delusion will actually take on convincing you that it is true that there is no truth or meaning as the purpose that gives meaning to their lives! This is not just ironic. It is also self-contradictory. It is self-referentially absurd. It cannot be true. Such people simply cannot be right.

Second, the world itself is full of clues that it is not just a mindless chance occurrence. It has not been here forever but came into existence out of nothing at a definite point of time in the finite past (the "Big Bang"). What could have caused that? You can't cause yourself to exist if you don't exist already. The world is also amazingly fine-tuned to make life possible. There are multiple factors such that none of them could be different from what they are by more than infinitesimal values without making it impossible for life to exist. It would be a pretty strange coincidence if that just happened by chance. And the world contains *information*—for example, the code of DNA. That is a very significant point that deserves some explanation.

Information is just not something that Nature can produce by random chance processes. If you are walking on the beach and see sand dollars arranged to spell out the English sentence "Beware of shark!" you do not conclude that random wave action washed them up in that pattern. Why? Waves don't know English phonics, English letters, English orthography (spelling), English lexicography (words), or English grammar. For anyone of those systems to have been reproduced randomly has odds that are vanishingly small. For them all to come together by chance to just happen to cooperate to produce an intelligible message? That is not going to happen. Some person—some intelligent agent—had to have done it for some reason, whether to warn you of shark activity or just to mess with your mind. DNA is like that. It is the same kind of coded *system*. So, who wrote that code? Hmmm.

The world makes more sense, then, if you see it as the creation of a personal God. But the third and most important reason Christians think that it is is that this God has revealed Himself in history through the incarnation of His Son as the man Jesus Christ. This is indicated by the fulfillment of many prophecies and by God having raised Him from the dead.[29] That resurrection is the best-attested event in ancient history. Even most skeptical and atheist historians admit that Jesus existed, that he was crucified, that he was buried in a borrowed grave, and that three days later that grave was empty. You then have to explain what happened to the body—and every explanation except one (that God raised Him) has fatal flaws and takes more faith to believe than the resurrection itself.[30]

---

[29] For much more information about all three of these reasons brought together in one place, see Douglas Groothuis, *Christian Apologetics: A Comprehensive Case for Biblical Faith* (Downers Grove, Il.: InterVarsity Press, 2011).

[30] See Frank Morison, *Who Moved the Stone?* (Downers Grove, Il.: InterVarsity Press, n.d.) for a classic defense of the historicity of the resurrection.

It is not just one line of evidence from nature or Scripture that convinces. It is the gestalt of all of them coming together, focused on the glory of God in the face of Jesus Christ. I've tried to summarize it thus:

Apologia

Structured Steps within the Dance,

Things that could not be by chance:

Architecture of belief?

Arch of bole and vein of leaf.

Crystal's angles, raindrops' curves,

Bone and sinew knit with nerves.

Flick of wrist, fly-toss, and then,

Break of bubble, flash of fin.

Beyond these sure and certain hints,

A clearer class of evidence:

Broken fever; opened eyes;

Dove descending from the skies.

Footstep firm on slope of wave;

Stone rolled back from Jesus' grave.

Glory growing out of grief?

Architecture of belief;

Things which could not be by chance:

Structured steps within the Dance.

Well, if all that is true, it changes everything. If a personal, intelligent, and purposeful God created the world and still cares for it enough to be involved with it, then good and evil are not just arbitrary values, and meaning and purpose can be more than wish fulfillment dreams. Bilbo was meant to find the Ring, and not by its maker—and that may indeed be an encouraging thought. It is encouraging, not just because it makes him feel better, but because it speaks truth about the real situation in the real world in which Frodo actually finds himself.

Tolkien and the Christian World View

Reading J. R. R. Tolkien can do two pretty wonderful things for people who are interested in understanding the Christian worldview. First, he shows us what it looks like when an intelligent and creative person has that worldview and applies it with confidence in his efforts to see, understand, and appreciate the world. The essay "On Fairie Stories" does it so well that it not only confirmed my hunches about the interpretation of *The Lord of the Rings* but showed me the difference a Christian worldview could make before I even knew that such a thing existed or what to call it. Tolkien's doctrine of sub-creation flows from the very heart of who God is and who we are: creative because we are made in the image of the Creator. I cannot help but agree with Clyde S. Kilby: "After years of teaching aesthetics, I cannot but conclude that the whole of that difficult subject is comprehended in a single line" from Tolkien's essay: "*We make still by the law in which we're made.*"[31] Tolkien got the starting point right, and few people have probed it more deeply.

Second, in his fiction, Tolkien gave us an endlessly fruitful lesson in how to see the world in the light of Christian truth. Middle Earth is *our* world interpreted mythically in terms of its deep past. It is thus just different enough from the world we live in in the Twentieth and

---

[31] Clyde S. Kilby, *Tolkien and the Silmarillion* (Wheaton: Harold Shaw, 1976), 54.

Twenty-First Centuries to let us see it afresh and let the disenchantment with it that Modernity has wrought in us be undone. We are thus able to experience the universe anew as a world of purposeful creation that allows darkness and light, the strength of dedicated weakness, significant sacrifice, personal providence, and Christlike heroes to have meaning again. Middle Earth becomes a lens through which we learn to see such things even in the contemporary world we inhabit.

One reason believers have loved *The Lord of the Rings* is that it reminds them that this is the way the world is. They feel it instinctively even when they don't make all of the connections that I began to make as a youth and have tried to bring out here. In a world that has lost confidence in those values, they need all the reminders they can get. And one reason I think many non-believers love the book is that it gives them an escape from a secular and meaningless world into a place where meaning and purpose not only exist but are believable. For that is a world in which their own natures are not frustrated but are fulfilled. And even if they don't believe that such a place can be real, they instinctively feel their need for it to exist. Tolkien awakens their homesickness and longing for a world in which meaning, and purpose are not illusions. And they cannot get enough of it.

Conclusion

Middle Earth is a world of meaning because it was sung into existence by Iluvatar and has not been abandoned by Him despite its corruption by evil. The real world is a world of meaning because it was spoken into existence by Yahweh and has not been abandoned by Him despite its corruption by evil. Thus Tolkien's writings are a set of corrective lenses that help to bring our own world into clearer focus for us. In *The Hobbit* and The *Lord of the Rings*, the Christian worldview is not on the surface where it's hard to miss, the way it is in C. S. Lewis's Narnia chronicles. But it is definitely there, as I have shown and as Tolkien himself confirmed.[32] As I put it once before, "Tolkien's book is as profoundly Christian as was the man himself. The Christian worldview of *The Lord of the Rings* is buried much deeper, below the surface, but its roots go down to the foundations of that world."[33]

In other words, Bilbo was meant to find the Ring, and not by its maker. If you need an encouraging thought, that would be a good place to start.

---

[32] "*The Lord of the Rings* is of course a fundamentally religious and Catholic work; unconsciously so at first, but consciously in the revision." Tolkien, *The Letters of J. R. R. Tolkien*, 172. Tolkien was of course a very devout Roman Catholic, and says that his story is not only Christian but Catholic. But while there are some Catholic elements for those who wish to look for them, fortunately the main Christian motifs, rooted in the biblical world view, as we have studied them here, are common to all faithful Christians of whatever denomination.

[33] Williams, *Mere Humanity*, 116.

INTERLUDE Naming

NAMING

And how he thought about them, trooping past,

    Stopping to lick his hand or sniff his knee--

    Tiny as a bee or hummingbird, or vast

    In girth the river-horse--and first to see

In fur and feather, clad heraldically,

    The colors--and the antics!--speechless, stare

    At scampering mice, at stallions' thunder, tree--

    Like limbs of elephants, ambling bulk of bear--

This creativity beyond compare--

    What fruit brought forth in bare but fertile mind;

    From sound and sight, throat muscles, subtle air,

    To weave the Words, the Poet's power unbind:

To call the Correspondences by name

    As Adam called the animals who came.

CHAPTER 3 "In the Beginning was the Word": Language and Creativity in Middle Earth

J. R. R. Tolkien was a *philologist*.[34] Yes, I spelled that word right. Not *philosopher*—though much of what we just said in the chapter on Tolkien and the Christian worldview might justify our using that word of him. He was by profession, by calling, by inclination, and by nature a philologist, and after his Christianity, there is hardly a more basic or important statement we could make about him. "I am a *pure* philologist," he once wrote. "I like history, and am moved by it, but its finest moments for me are those when it throws light upon words."[35] But what does *philology* mean?

Philology is not a word we encounter much anymore. The hyper-specialization of the modern academy has not been kind to philology. There you will find linguists, people who study language, and there you will find literary scholars, people who study literature; and seldom will the two meet. But a philologist is a person who is concerned with both: with literature from the standpoint of its language and with language as it appears in literature, particularly the history of words. So Tolkien said that his goal was "to advance, to the best of my ability, the growing neighborliness of linguistic and literary studies, which can never be enemies except by misunderstanding or without loss to both."[36] Thus philology is essential to the study of literature, especially of literature that is old

---

[34] See Scull and Hammond, *The J. R. R. Tolkien Companion and Guide* (Boston: Houghton Mifflin, 2006), 2:754f, for a history of the word, its usage, and the development of philology as an academic field in relation to Tolkien's place in it..

[35] Tolkien, *Letters*, 264.

[36] Ibid., 13.

enough so that its readers can no longer take its grammar or the meaning of its words for granted.[37]

My students get a wee taste of philology when I try to explain to them that in Shakespeare's time the distinction between formal and informal pronouns that they have encountered in Spanish was still part of the English language (*thou* corresponding to Spanish *tu*, and *you* to *usted*), or that this or that word they think they know has undergone specialization, or generalization, or amelioration, or pejoration of meaning since the early Seventeenth Century. It makes a difference. Changes in the meaning of words make an obvious difference in interpretation, but the subtleties of grammar are much more exciting. When Kent asks Lear, "What wouldst thou do, old man?" we understand how upset he must be at the king's folly in disinheriting Cordelia by his losing his self-control so far as to use the informal pronoun *thou* with the King instead of the more polite *you*. Without philology—literature understood from the standpoint of the history of its language—you would miss that nuance completely.

Sometimes philology changes interpretation; sometimes it just enables it. (I'm not sure which is more important.) I can't resist going on about the fact that there used to be more n-plurals (like our *oxen* or *brethren*) on words like *eye-eyen*, *tree-treen*, and *shoe-shoon*. Understanding the impersonal verb ("It likes me" = "I like it"), the lack of a group genitive ("The duke's niece of Gloucester" = "The duke of Gloucester's niece"), and the more flexible word order of Elizabethan English helps Shakespeare's language seem less foreign. Learning that there were more case endings in the personal pronouns

---

[37] See Tom Shippey, *The Road to Middle Earth: How J. R. R. Tolkien Created a New Mythology* (London: Allen & Unwin, 1982), chapter one, "Lit. and Lang.," for what may be the best explanation in print of philology as conceived and practiced by Tolkien.

back then (*thou* = subjective, *thy* possessive, *thee* objective case; i.e., you use *thou* for the subject of the sentence and *thee* for the direct object, indirect object, or the object of a preposition: "*Thou* art my reader; I am writing to *thee*") and more endings not yet lost in the verb conjugations (I *do*, thou *dost*, he *doth*—you don't just add *est* to all the verbs willy-nilly) gives us greater competence and confidence in what we are reading. We have philology to thank for all of that.

My students get a somewhat heavier dose of philology when I try to enable them to read Chaucer's Middle English, for which they have to understand everything I said about Shakespeare and much more besides. I can't resist waxing lyrical about the Great Vowel Shift (why we have to learn new values for the vowels when we learn Spanish or French—they kept the old sounds when English changed them—and in Chaucer's day English was still using the original sounds). I revel in the pronunciation of syllables that have since gone silent and what that does to the music of Chaucer's verse. "*Whan that Aprille his shoures soote / The droughte of Marche hath perced to the roote / And bathed everye veine in swich licour / Of which vertu engendered is the flour. . . .*" Don't get me started! No doubt to my poor students it seems as if I could go on forever, but I know I can't. It makes me sad that I can only wade in the shallows of the great ocean in which Tolkien was a deep-sea diver. At least I can admire some of the pearls he and his fellow philologists brought to the surface.

What has all this got to do with the Christian worldview in Tolkien's fiction? Everybody notices how good his names are, and how appropriate they sound to the people and places they refer to. That is not an accident, nor is it a trivial factor in the beauty of his writing. It flows directly from his philology.[38] But the world-view connection runs much deeper than just sonorous and appropriate names. It is indeed the very foundation on which those names are built. As Verlyn Flieger rightly notes, "Words were for Tolkien not just a window into the past but the key to that lost relationship between man and God of which our sense of the Fall is our only memory."[39] She adds, "This connection between mind, language, and story is of special importance to Tolkien's mythology, for it is the basis of his myth and the genesis of his fiction."[40] The point of connection is the doctrine of sub-creation from the essay "On Fairie Stories": We are creative because we are made in the image of the Creator. And for Tolkien, the philologist, the place where that creativity shows up most profoundly is not in the Fairy Stories themselves, actually, but in something even older and more basic to our divinely imaged human nature: in language itself.

As you are probably not a philologist, you may not have noticed how even the most simple human speech involves a nexus of creativity unparalleled in the natural world or in non-linguistic human experience. You don't have to be a great verbal artist; the mere fact that you are able to speak at all makes you a creative genius. If you are not yet sufficiently awed by the profound depths of which

---

[38] "Behind my stories," he wrote, "is a nexus of languages. [The elves have] two related languages more nearly completed, whose history is written, and whose forms (representing two different sides of my own linguistic taste) are deduced scientifically from a common origin. Out of these languages are made nearly all the names that appear in my legends. This gives a certain character (a cohesion, a consistency of linguistic style, and an illusion of historicity) to the nomenclature, or so I believe, that is markedly lacking in other comparable things." *Letters*, 143.

[39] *Splintered Light: Logos and Language in Tolkien's World* (Grand Rapids: Eerdmans, 1983), 9. Flieger has an excellent discussion of how Tolkien's essays on Beowulf and on Fairie Stories relate to his world view and his fiction.

[40] Ibid., 23-4.

the human mind is capable through the mystery of human creativity, ponder the fact that you have just successfully read this sentence. It has quite a complex structure, with an independent clause and three subordinate clauses, plus four prepositional phrases. It contains thirty different words used thirty-seven times. (We won't even try to think about the phonemes and morphemes—don't tempt me!) Five of the thirty words get multiple uses: the personal pronoun *you*, the preposition *of*, forms of the verb *to be*, and the adjective *human* appear twice each, the article *the* four times; twenty-five words are used once each.

Now, the odds that you have ever seen these exact words before combined in precisely that order are, for all practical purposes, zero (unless you have read my earlier book *Mere Humanity*, in which I use the same illustration). I could spend a whole chapter just analyzing that one sentence without taxing my own patience (yours is another matter). Yet I created the sentence effortlessly, and most of you probably understood it with little or no conscious effort. Both of those facts are just plain stupefying. And usually, we do not even waste the adjective *creative* on expository prose of the kind I am writing now! But without this almost indescribable human capacity for creativity, language could not work. You see, without consciously doing any of the formal analysis (until after the fact), I spontaneously *created* a structure that allowed you to *recreate* with some accuracy in your mind the fairly complex and sophisticated meaning I was attending to in mine.

Man's creation in the image of God (the *imago Dei*) is, of course, the source of the difference between us and the rest of the animal creation. But what is the *imago Dei*, exactly? Is it our amphibious nature combining matter and spirit, our rationality, our moral (or immoral) nature, our capacity for relationship with God, or is it simply the position we occupy as His regents, representing Him as the stewards and governors of His creation? None of these attributes is irrelevant to the *imago*, but neither is any of them its essence. Theologians can spend interminable pages debating the details to no purpose because they have never bothered to read Genesis for its narrative flow in context. When we do, the answer is very plain.

The first statement in Scripture that God intends to create Man in His own image occurs very early, in Genesis 1:26. We are in the first chapter of the first book of the Bible. So, let us start from scratch. So far, we have only seen two attributes of God in action; they are all that has been revealed to this point, hence all we know of Him. First, He is creative; second, He is articulate. And these two facts are related: He uses language as the means of His creativity, first declaring things into existence and then giving them both form (separating light and darkness, water and land, etc.) and value (it was very good). So if we are then told that Man is going to be "like" God, one would think that this likeness must refer to the only attributes that have so far been introduced into the narrative. Man too will be creative and articulate, and in a way that transcends those capacities as they appear in rudimentary form in the lower animals.

Then this reasonable assumption is confirmed by the story. Adam is the first creature to be *personally* addressed by God's speech; after a long string of third-person "let there be's" he is called "thou." And he immediately starts talking back. His first official act is to *create* the first human *language*: God brings the animals before him, and whatever Adam calls each one is its name. God accepts these names Adam has created and will graciously use them Himself. So, Man, like God, is creative, and creative because he is articulate, creative by means of his articulation. The core of the *imago Dei* is language.

61

This view of the *imago* is also confirmed by what we know of language itself. It is a uniquely human creation, the one that makes all the others possible. Scientists debate whether chimps can be taught to use true language, either using Ameslan (American Sign Language for the Deaf, as with Washoe) or computers (at the Yerkes Primate Center at Emory University in Atlanta, for example). But the forms of communication these apes are observed to use in the wild do not have the open-endedness, the deep structure, or the creativity required of a true human language. Rather, they are locked into an instinctual system that does not easily grow or develop. They can possibly be gotten to move beyond that natural instinctive system by their keepers, but they do not have an innate drive to do so like we do.

A given troupe of monkeys in the wild, in other words, might have a fairly large "vocabulary" of sounds that are meaningful to the life of monkey: "food," "danger," "I'll pick your ticks off if you pick mine." But they do not make up new sounds that have new meanings that have never before entered into the mind of a monkey. They do not rearrange the old sounds into new patterns to communicate new and more sophisticated ideas that have never before entered into the mind of a monkey. Human beings do that all the time, without even thinking about it. This incredible *creativity* with sound is what separates human language from even the most sophisticated and impressive forms of animal communication. It is the one trait that is uniquely and specifically *human*, and the source of all the others. If the higher apes have learned to speak, in other words, it is only after Man has been messing around with their minds. We are still the only creature who creates language spontaneously. The uniqueness of language as a human characteristic is therefore not ultimately threatened by these experiments.

Notice the key phrase I used repeatedly above: Man "*creates* language." For creativity is precisely what separates human language from other forms of animal communication. The famous dance of the honey bees conveys some pretty impressive information: the precise distance and direction from the hive in which lies the field of clover. But the bees are locked into the steps that tell the other bees this. Again, they never come up with a new dance step or a new combination of steps to communicate a new idea that has never before entered into the mind of the bee. Human beings do that all the time. They do it so effortlessly that they are often not even aware of it. Hundreds of new words are coined and introduced into the English language every year. But it's not just new words. Do you remember the sentence we analyzed a few paragraphs above? Or just substitute for it any of the sentences you are reading now. How about the next one? *Creativity*, in other words, the fact that neither I as a writer nor you as a reader are locked into a set of instinctual patterns from which we cannot deviate, is what allowed me to compose this sentence and you to understand it.

The miracle (I do not use the word lightly) of language allows us to contemplate things, objects, and ideas, not immediately present in the physical environment, and then to manipulate them in our heads. It is, therefore, the foundation of our capacity for abstract thinking and reason. Language allows us to render an account to God of our stewardship of His creation. It is, therefore, the foundation of the fact that, in a manner not true of the other animals, we are *accountable* for our actions, i.e., have a moral nature. That accountability allows us to function as His regents, the stewards of creation. We see then that all the major facets of our uniqueness that have traditionally been related to the image of God find their unity in language; it is the characteristic we share with Him that makes all the others possible. Like Him, we are creative and articulate, articulately creative and creatively articulate. We are language users because we are language makers, made in the image of the Word.[41]

It is, therefore, no accident that the greatest storyteller of the Twentieth Century, who propounded as well as practiced the theory of sub-creation, began the creation of the most believable, consistent, and compelling imaginary world ever known with the ultimate act of human creativity: the endeavor to create a language.[42] Yes. Tolkien, the philologist, did not set out to create an imaginary world and then use his expertise in philology to give it nice-sounding names. What he wanted to do was make his own *language*, one that would not just be a personal code but have the feel, the grammar, the deep structure, of an actual language like the ones he had been studying: Latin, Greek Old English, Old Norse, Sanskrit, Gothic, Finnish. What he produced was what we now know as Elvish. "Nobody believes me," he protested, "when I say that my long book is an attempt to create a world in which a form of language agreeable to my personal aesthetic might seem real. . . . It was an effort to create a situation in which a common greeting would be *elen sila lumen omentielmo*",[43] which means "A star shines on the hour of our meeting."

An actual language is a living and growing system which is the sum total of the creative input of each of its speakers, tempered by the creative input of all the others, to produce a shared set of dynamic conventions they can

---

[41] See Donald T. Williams, *Inklings of Reality: Essays Toward a Christian Philosophy of Letters*, 2nd ed. (Lynchburg: Lantern Hollow Press, 2012), chapter one, for further discussion of these points.

[42] See Tom Shippey, "Creation from Philology in *The Lord of the Rings*." in Salu, Mary and Robert T. Farrell, eds., *J. R. R. Tolkien, Scholar and Storyteller: Essays* in Memoriam (Ithaca: Cornell Univ. Pr., 1979), 286-316, for brilliant analysis of some of the details of that process.

[43] Tolkien, *Letters*, 264.

use for real communication. No committee of experts sits around in an ivory tower somewhere and makes it up. It grows without a plan as real people, along with other real people, respond with all their God-given creativity to their needs for communication in a particular landscape with a particular set of problems, challenges, opportunities, and beauties. So Tolkien discovered that in order for Elvish to have a convincing sense of reality *as a language*, it required a people to speak it. That people would need a world to live in. Their existence in that world would have to include a history and a mythology for them to remember and other languages (spoken by neighboring peoples, who would have all the same requirements) for their speech to be related to. And that is why Elvish ended up with two historical forms, Quenya and Sindarin, and why it pulled Dwarfish, Numenorean, Westron, the Black Speech, and Orcish into the world with it, along with those peoples and their lands and their cultures and their deeds. That is why Tolkien's fantasy world can seem more like a real place than cities we have actually visited or lived in.

It all began with language. Tolkien made Middle Earth because he was made in the image of the God who *spoke* the world into existence. I doubt he came up with the doctrine of sub-creation and then decided to put it into practice. "Hmmm. Man creates because he is made in the image of the Creator who created with language; therefore . . . I know! I shall become a philologist and create Middle Earth based on the foundation of language." No. No doubt he simply followed his heart and the explanation of what he had done came later. He was working on the languages of Middle Earth long before he had any idea of the stories they would generate. It was done with astounding dedication in the midst of and in spite of the horrors of the Great War—"in grimy canteens, at lectures in cold fogs, in huts full of blasphemy and smut, or by candlelight in bell-tents, even some down in dugouts under shell fire."[44] The explanation came later, but it was not any worse an explanation for that. Seldom has there been a tighter fit between theory and practice, seldom a philosophy of life lived out more thoroughly and more profoundly.

And what were the elements of that philosophy? Everything begins with a personal and articulate and creative God. In the beginning was the Word. Man is made in the image of that God. That is why human beings make stories out of language, and that is why those stories have meaning. God spoke and from that speaking came the world. Tolkien explored the depths of language; he learned to speak Elvish; and from that speaking came Middle Earth.

Not all creative writers have to make a language to make a world, even a good one. They do all create a world with its own laws, history, etc., as a setting for their own characters. They create that world and then determine the laws of its nature, which they then have to follow consistently if their story is going to have the "inner consistency of reality" Tolkien spoke of in his essay.[45] They can make a world where various kinds of magic are possible, or where warp speed works if they like. (Even people who write so-called "realistic" fiction are doing this; they simply choose to have the same natural laws, etc., as the real world.) They are all acting out the image of God when they do so, creating in the image of the Creator. Tolkien was simply doing it on an even more profound level by starting with language itself. That is why Middle Earth has the grounded sense of reality that other writers can only envy. We feel that The Shire *must* be there, and we want to visit it.

---

[44] Tolkien, Letters, 78.

[45] "On Fairie Stories," *The Tolkien Reader*, op. cit., 47f.

We see then that a confluence of three mighty rivers gave us the Mississippi of Middle Earth. First was Tolkien the Christian, who had thought about doctrines like the Gospel, Creation, and Christ as the *Logos* (the Word) because he held them as really true and used them to understand the world. Second was Tolkien the philologist who thought deeply about the nature of language and could not stop in his wrestling with it until he had created languages that truly mirrored linguistic reality. Third was Tolkien the creative writer, who dipped his ladle deep into the Cauldron of Story and came up with a new mythology. All three of these tributaries flowed together in one mighty stream in the creation of Tolkien's fiction. And so, the Elves sail down Anduin to the sea.

The nature of such creativity needs nothing less than a sonnet to try to capture it adequately. Here's an attempt:

SOME REAL MAGIC

Within the cadences of human speech,

Attentive listeners can sometimes hear

The rhythm of the wave upon the beach

Or contemplate the music of the spheres.

Within the small sphere of the human eye,

The watcher who knows how to look can see

A spirit that's as lofty as the sky

Or humble as the lover on his knee.

When in the alembic of the human mind

Imagination boils with memory,

Such vision with such sound can be combined,

Far more mysterious than alchemy!

The Philosopher's Stone we vainly sought of old

Could never have made such rare and costly gold.

I'm not, of course, saying you have to be a philologist to be a Christian or a creative writer. But if your worldview flows from the affirmation that "In the beginning was the Word" (John 1:1), you should have an understanding of language and its significance that will enhance your appreciation for how God used Tolkien to bring the Christian worldview to such powerful expression. You will see that every time a human being opens his mouth, he is giving testimony to the existence of God—even if what comes out of it is arguments for atheism or curses or blasphemy. You will appreciate in a new way why the *Lord of the Rings* is such a masterpiece. Its author was uniquely gifted to practice what he preached. And so his fiction flowed from his philology, and both from his belief in the God whose language was the creation of the world.

We are all differently gifted, and possibly no one will ever be able to be gifted as Tolkien was again. The loss of a classical education that starts with acquiring competence in the classical languages makes it very unlikely. Nevertheless, we should all take our own gifts, such as they are and find ways to practice what we preach, to live out our worldview. We won't be able to do it in quite the way Tolkien did. But may we be granted to do it as faithfully.

INTERLUDE The Origin of Language

Then Man, the wielder   of Words, awoke,
Saw the sunlight   slanting down,
Saw the ground-fog   swelling upward,
Heard the light   laughter of leaves,
Climbed the mountains,   mist-enshrouded,
Felt the wind,   wet with rain,
Saw the stabbing   stars in darkness,
Watched the antics of   wild creatures,
Heard within his   head the sounds,
Pulled them forth,   in patterns ordered,
Uttered into   air around him
Liquid Names;   in lilting language,
Spoke the mighty   Spell of Speech.

Chapter 4 "You're not Telling it Right!" Peter Jackson's Betrayal of J. R. R. Tolkien's Vision

"If therefore they say to you, 'Behold, he is in the wilderness,' do not go forth, or, 'Behold, he is in the inner rooms,' do not believe them." (Mat. 24:26)

Introduction

The books or the movies?

The popularity of Peter Jackson's movie versions of Tolkien's story and the fact that at certain points he did an excellent job of recreating Middle Earth make this a question that has to be asked. Yet at certain other very critical points the two visions of Tolkien's story just are not the same. Anyone who has only seen the movies without reading the books will get a distorted picture of what Tolkien's story is all about. Such a person, for example, would not get nearly as clear a picture of the five biblical motifs as the one I got from reading the books as a teenager and tried to explain here in chapter one.

All of us who have had small children and have read or told them stories know that their appetite for hearing a favorite one again is nearly insatiable, far more insatiable, usually, than our appetite for telling it. So parents have all come to that moment when we felt that any variation at all from the familiar pattern would be a blessed relief. Thus Goldilocks, after her disappointment with the first two bowls of porridge, gives up and leaves the third bowl untasted. But we never get to the wonderfully creative new tangent this omission has made possible, for we are interrupted by the plaintive cry, "You're not telling it right!"

Are our children hidebound purists who wish to squelch our creativity? No. They know the difference between making up our own story and telling one that has already been established, and they will appreciate the creativity involved in making up our own when we exercise it in its proper sphere. And they may not know, but they sense, that there is a good reason why Goldilocks needs to sample that third bowl, for the violation of the original pattern cannot be expected to produce really satisfactory results. So perhaps the great tragedy of Peter Jackson's second and third installments of his film version of Tolkien's *The Lord of the Rings* is that his own children were too young to have yet read the original work for themselves. They might have saved you the necessity of reading this chapter!

General Comments

In *The Fellowship of the Ring*, the first film in the trilogy, most of the changes from Tolkien's original tale can be defended as necessary simplifications required by the translation of the richer medium, books, into the more limited one, movies. (I say that the book is a richer medium because it engages the reader's imagination to help create the images rather than supplying them ready made and because it can move at a more leisurely pace, making greater detail in the realization of the story possible.) But, starting with the second installment, Jackson's departures from the original story become increasingly more difficult to justify.

The problem with these movies is actually that Peter Jackson has done so many things so very well. The orcs are the first I've seen who actually look like what they are, the twisted and deformed descendants of ruined elves. The landscapes are mostly magnificent in their appropriateness. The battles are well realized, if not entirely accurate. The Ents' bodies are well portrayed, even

71

if their character lacks the full depth that lay behind Treebeard's eyes. Sam Gamgee's character, on the other hand, is drawn as perfectly as one could ask for (until one unfortunate scene in *The Return of the King*, of which more anon). Gollum moves and acts (mostly) like Gollum. The architecture is mostly splendid: Hobbiton is Hobbiton, Bag End is Bag End, Meduseld is Meduseld, Orthanc is Orthanc, Minas Tirith is Minas Tirith, and Barad Dur is Barad Dur. (The one exception is Rivendell, which looks more like an abode for Sugar Plum Fairies than for Eldar.) The acting (with the unfortunate but crucial exception of Elijah Wood's Frodo) is mostly tolerable to good.

Jackson even makes one change to the plot of *The Lord of the Rings* that actually makes sense, indeed, better sense than the book. It is in *The Fellowship of the Ring* when instead of having Aragorn carrying a useless sword on his journeys, Anduril is shown as being kept in a shrine in Rivendell. Tolkien has Aragorn pull out half of the sword at Bree to help Sam connect him to the sword that was broken in the rhyme. It makes dramatic sense in that scene until you stop to think about it. Aragorn is the greatest outdoorsman, tracker, and hunter in the world. Anybody who has done any backpacking at all knows that the last thing an experienced hiker is going to do is carry around dead weight, and the last thing a man hunted by a dangerous enemy is going to do is carry around a sword he can't use to defend himself. So along with some innocent changes required by the adaptation to a new medium, there is one that is actually an improvement. It is, I'm afraid, the exception that proves the rule.

So why are all these real excellences a problem? Because all this is in fact done so well, at such expense, and with so much profit, that it is hard to imagine that anybody will ever be given a chance to do another, more faithful version of *The Lord of the Rings*. So, you can't just hate it and be done with it, the way you could, say, Bakshi's version from the 1970's. We're stuck with having to deal with these movies; we cannot just dismiss them. Unfortunately, this means that our hatred of Jackson's betrayals (of Faramir, Arwen, and Denethor, and through them of Tolkien) must, therefore, be all the more intense. *Betrayals?* That is a strong word. I will justify my use of it before I am done.

We must be content to see the story simplified. That is unavoidable when making any long and rich book into a movie, even a nine-hour epic. So, I didn't so much mind Tom Bombadil disappearing or even Arwen replacing Glorfindel in the first installment. (As most of the changes in the first film were of this nature, we don't need to say much more about it here.) Thus, I don't think I am being an unreasonable "purist" when I say that to change the basic nature, personality, and motivation of a major character is just unacceptable, and that to do so and still claim to be making a movie of *The Lord of the Rings* is simply dishonest.

The Two Towers

Some of the changes in *The Two Towers* are more annoyances than betrayals. Having the Ents not make the right decision about Saruman so they have to be tricked into it by Merry and Pippin (who, according to the movie itself, could not have known about the devastation they show Treebeard because they had not passed through that part of Fangorn) was a wholly unnecessary "plothole." The stupid "exorcism" of Theoden (who "youthens" way too much as a result, by the way--he should still be an old man afterward), rather than Tolkien's more subtle scene is an irritation. I would much rather have seen the Huorns at Helm's Deep than to have Eomer (who was already supposed to be there) come charging up with his army, but I suppose I can live with the battle we were offered.

But some of the changes are neither credible, nor acceptable, nor even tolerable. The worst sins in *The Two Towers* are as follows. The first is having Arwen head off to the Grey Havens (and Aragorn believe that she is doing so), thus setting up a much deeper entanglement between Aragorn and Eowyn than Tolkien ever intended or would have tolerated. Elrond is much too wise to try to escape his fate, however costly. To interfere with a union that is necessary for the future of Middle Earth through such a self-serving plan is totally out of character for him. The idea that Arwen would even consider going back on her oath to Aragorn, no matter what the cost, is just plain sickening, as is the idea that he assumes she would. That is not the woman the king of men loved; that is not the king of men. A solid integrity basic to both characters and to their love story has just disappeared, and we hardly recognize them as a result.

The second problem is like the first. It is the loss of the clear contrast between the characters of Boromir and Faramir. The original Faramir said he wouldn't have picked the Ring up if he found it lying on the road.[46] Not exactly what the character in the movie says: "Tell my father Faramir sends him a powerful weapon." The original Faramir showed his quality to Sam, and it was "the very highest."[47] That contrast was something Tolkien wanted to show us—but Jackson declined to do so. Why the difference? As with Aragorn and Arwen, uncomplicated nobility is apparently beyond anything Jackson can imagine. He feels obligated to complicate such characters, whether because he thinks they are unbelievable or undramatic. But Tolkien understood the importance of imagining uncompromised virtue, of the need for images of goodness to contrast with images of evil. Compared to the character in the book, the movie Faramir is, again,

---

[46] Tolkien, *The Two Towers*, 330.

[47] Ibid, 343.

simply unrecognizable. There seems to be a pattern emerging here.

The third problem is Gollum's too easy "conversion." The good side of Gollum (call it Smeagol) tells the bad side (Gollum) to "Go away and never come back," and it apparently does so until Gollum feels betrayed at Henneth Annun. In the books, the difference between the two sides of Gollum's character is much more subtle. Tolkien's Gollum is a more complicated and conflicted character, with greater potential for both good *and* evil, than the figure in the movie. Gollum's internal conflict may have been harder to portray in the medium of film, but a greater effort was needed. This is a serious flaw because it makes the mortal will seem much more autonomous, much more able to just up and decide things unrooted in its habits and history, than it is in reality.

The bottom line is that Tolkien shows us a more profound vision of both good and evil than Jackson is apparently capable of. The changes Jackson made to these characters all have the effect of blunting the contrast between good and evil. In the end, they do nothing more than gin up superfluous dramatic conflict by sacrificing both credibility and faithfulness.

The Return of the King

The pre-release internet buzz was that Peter Jackson's third installment of his version of the Tolkien trilogy stayed closer to the book than his *The Two Towers*. That is true only in a very gross and superficial sense. There was, it is true, only one *new* big departure from the original plot (of which more in a moment). What we have instead, though, is the inevitable workings out of the altered plot arcs caused by the disastrous big departures made in *The Two Towers*. But there were a thousand *little* changes, which, like Chinese water torture, make it almost impossible to enjoy the good things in the film (e.g., one of the best artistic renderings of Minas Tirith ever). These little changes also reveal, as clearly as the major departures in the second movie, the shallowness of Jackson's understanding of Tolkien's Christian worldview and therefore of his epic.

Once again, I will say nothing here against the omissions and conflations of plot elements, as much as we would all have liked to see the scouring of the Shire. Some simplification has to be expected in an adaptation, and anyone who won't accept that just shouldn't watch movies based on books. What is troubling are the thousand and one little *gratuitous* changes to the original that served no good purpose. No doubt, again, they were intended to make things more dramatic on screen and/or to bring out elements of the conflict as Jackson sees them. But almost every one of these unnecessary changes is either a clumsy and heavy-handed treatment of themes Tolkien showed us with much greater skill and subtlety, is just plain pointless and stupid, or betrays an appalling lack of understanding of what Tolkien was doing (and why) when he wrote the story the way he did.

Here are some of the changes that were not helpful. A few typical examples of these gratuitous changes to the plot in *The Return of the King* will have to suffice; no doubt you can think of many more. One thinks of Pippin sneaking off to light the Beacons of Gondor—as if the Rohirrim weren't going to be summoned otherwise. Gandalf punching out Denethor with his staff was simply demeaning to both characters. The movie Denethor has none of the nobility that made his fall tragic in the book; he is just a dottering and despicable old fool rather than a great and noble Greek tragic hero destroyed by *hubris.* Finally, Sam beating the snot out of a supine and passive Gollum is absurd on two counts. Not only would he have been physically incapable of this—it took both Frodo and

Sam to subdue Gollum, and then only with the threat of Sting and the influence of the Ring—but, knowing that Gollum was under Frodo's protection, it is just not something Sam would have done, no matter how strong his feelings. It was completely out of character—as was Frodo telling Sam to "Go home."

Finally, we have a seemingly small but actually hugely consequential change. In the book, Frodo yields at last to the temptation to claim the Ring as his own and refuses to destroy it by throwing it into the cracks of doom. But in a powerfully ironic twist, Gollum, who has no intention of destroying the Ring, attacks Frodo on the edge of the cliff above the fire and bites off his finger to reclaim the Ring. Then in his dance of joyful celebration, he takes one step too far and falls over the cliff, causing the Ring to be destroyed after all despite Frodo's weakness and his own malice. But in the movie, Frodo *pushes* Gollum off the cliff at the climax of their struggle. It is more dramatic that way. But what does it do to the theme?

Jackson turns an accident into an act. Presumably, he does so because the scene is more "dramatic" that way. But substituting the act for the accident seriously diminishes Tolkien's emphasis on the role of Providence (or, to use his own words, "Luck, if luck you call it"). The outcome of the book does not result from the act or the intention of either character, but from something much closer to fate or destiny. Frodo's failure to destroy the Ring himself and Gollum's playing the unintentional part Gandalf had predicted for him is a moment prepared for by many plot elements carefully set up throughout the work, as we showed here in chapter one. It is the promised outworking of Gandalf's insight that there was something bigger at work in the history of the Ring, that Bilbo had been *meant* to find it, and not by its maker. Readers of *The Silmarillion* will realize that Iluvatar has been at work all the way through and that this is why Gandalf's words may be "an encouraging thought." Jackson's change, his substitution of act for apparent accident, muddies the clarity Tolkien had labored so hard to set up. It thus sacrifices significance for excitement and dilutes the meaning Tolkien had been setting up for a thousand pages. It is the ultimate triumph over the text of Jackson's failure to grasp what Tolkien was really about in the composition of the work.

What Is Going On?

Why does Peter Jackson do it? You would expect him to simplify the story--the switch to the medium of film demands that—but Jackson actually gratuitously complicates things! A very fundamental problem seems to me to lie behind these changes. It is Jackson's failure to grasp the depths of Tolkien's Christian worldview as we laid it out in chapter one. He cannot comprehend the depths of the hold that sin has on us—hence, for example, Smeagol telling Gollum to "leave now, and never come back." Too easy, too simple, a clumsy handling of what Tolkien does much more believable and subtly in portraying the same inner conflict. Gollum's hand hesitantly reaching out to caress Frodo is more subtle, more believable (because it does not necessarily imply that Slinker and Stinker are as neatly separable as the movie's version makes them), and, as interrupted by the misunderstanding Sam, more tragic. Why? Because Tolkien understood the biblical doctrine of sin too well to imagine that one can even temporarily banish one's evil side by simply telling it to get lost.

Ironically, the failure to appreciate the true depths of evil also makes it impossible for Jackson to believe in the real potential human beings have on the other side, for heroism and integrity. One's ability to appreciate sin and capacity to understand grace inevitably go hand in hand. So good characters like Faramir (or Aragorn, or Arwen) are felt to be *too* good to be believable, and hence have to be "complicated." That is how we get an Aragorn who, instead of faithfully pursuing his calling, is resisting the kingship because he fears he will repeat the tragic error of Isildur. And we have a Faramir who initially is much more like his brother than the one in the book. As a result, the movie Faramir, like the movie Gollum, also has (ironically) a cheap and unmotivated conversion. What is it about the attack of the Nazgul at Osgiliath that suddenly makes him think it is a good idea to send Frodo and Sam off into Mordor alone? That is a decision Tolkien's Faramir could make in Tolkien's scene, but not one that this Faramir can make believably in Jackson's scene.

Two Philosophies of Literature

Let's probe the differences between the books and the movies a bit further. Why do the books and the movies of *The Lord of the Rings* seem to present two such different worlds, not physically but in terms of their moral vision? A sixteenth-century treatise on literary criticism, Sir Philip Sidney's "Defense of Poesy" (or "Apology for Poetry"), further explains some of the discrepancies between J. R. R. Tolkien's and Peter Jackson's views of their task.

Sidney articulates an older vision of literature that Tolkien shared and built on. It is an explicitly Christian vision. By *Poet*, Sidney and other writers before him meant any creative writer, not just a writer of verse; etymologically *poetry* is from the Greek *poiein*, "to make." So any writer of fiction is a poet and any fictional story a poem by that definition. "The Defense of Poesy" is then a defense of creative writing of any kind, including but not limited to what we would call poetry.

Sidney starts from Plato's discussion of poetry in *The Republic*, so we had better start by explaining a bit about Plato's philosophy. Here is a basic question he dealt with:

79

What are more real, ideas or things? Most of us probably think that things are real and that ideas are pictures of things that we have in our heads. Plato had it just the other way around. For him, the idea (what he called the Form) is the ultimate reality, and the things we see in nature are imperfect copies or imitations of those perfect ideas showing up in our experience. Whether Plato was right about that is a difficult question. If we think of the Forms as existing in the mind of God, it's hard not to think there is some truth in Plato's view. A Christian could develop a version of Platonism that avoids some of its errors, which flow from the fact that Plato did not know of a personal God, and so had no place for his theoretical Ideas to exist. (Augustine found the solution: they are the *rationes aeternae*, the eternal ideas in the mind of God.) For our purposes here, the problem is not so much Plato's view of Ideas as the application of them he made to literature and its writers.

Plato had banned poets from his ideal state. Why? It had to do with Plato's notion of literature as an art of imitation. Fiction, Plato assumes, imitates nature. But nature is already an imitation of the Ideas or the Forms, which in Plato's philosophy are the ultimate reality. So that makes fiction an imitation of an imitation. Thus, it is taking you one step further from the truth. Fiction is a lie by definition, not just because the events it narrates didn't actually happen, but because as an imitation of an imitation it cannot represent reality well in any sense. Therefore, poetry or fiction is not a proper subject for the instruction of the youth who will become Plato's future citizens and Philosopher Kings.

But Sidney the Christian realized that something much more profound is going on. The creative writer does not merely, as Hamlet put it, "hold the mirror up to nature." He is not just an imitator—the function that had caused Plato to banish the Poets and their fictions from his ideal state. The Poet is not just slavishly and imperfectly imitating nature. Here's how Sidney puts it: "Disdaining any such subjection, lifted up with the vigor of his own invention, [the Poet] doth grow in effect another nature, in making things either better than nature bringeth forth, or quite anew."[48] In other words, because he is free to invent characters and events that do not actually exist in nature and history, the Poet can give you a character who is a better example of virtue (or vice) than nature could produce. The Poet may thus actually take us closer to divine truth, rather than further from it, than fallen nature can. (Because he is also fallen he may give us false and corrupting images instead; but *usum abusus non tollit*, the abuse of his creative power does not overturn the right use of it.) The Poet has this potential to surpass nature in embodying the truth because he is created in the image of the Creator. We should therefore "give right honor to the Maker of that maker, who, having made man to his own likeness, set him beyond and over all the works of that second nature; which in nothing he showeth so much as in poetry, when with the force of a divine breath he brings things forth far surpassing her doings."[49]

Tolkien follows Sidney explicitly, for in his essay "On Fairie Stories" he develops Sidney's insight and brings it to completion in his own doctrine of "sub-creation": Man is creative because he is made in the image of the Creator.

Used or misused, [our] right has not decayed:

We make still by the law in which we're made.[50]

One of Sidney's applications of this Christian theory of literature helps to explain the difference between

---

[48] Sir Philip Sidney, "The Defense of Poesy (1595)," in Hyder E. Rollins and Herschel Baker, eds., *The Renaissance in England* (Lexington, MA: D. C. Heath, 1954), 607.

[49] Ibid., 608.

[50] Tolkien, *The Tolkien Reader*, 54.

Tolkien's and Jackson's versions of Tolkien's legendarium. For one of the things that the Poet can potentially do better than nature is to embody truth more faithfully in ways that are more than just intellectual. The Poet, argues Sidney, achieves the end or purpose of learning, "virtuous action," better than either the Historian or the Philosopher. The Historian gives you a concrete story you can relate to, but he is limited to what has actually been done; he cannot (as a historian) tell you what *ought* to be done. The moral Philosopher speaks of the ideal, but does it so abstractly that the average reader cannot follow it— the Philosopher is "so hard of utterance and misty to be conceived, that one that hath no other guide but him shall wade in him until he be old before he shall find sufficient cause to be honest."[51] So the Philosopher has the precept, and the Historian the example—but "both, not having both, do both halt [i.e., stumble]."[52] They stumble and fall short of the ultimate goal of education: inspiring and enabling virtuous action on the part of the reader himself.

But look, says Sidney, what the Poet can do:

> Now doth the peerless Poet perform both. For whatsoever the Philosopher saith should be done, [the Poet] giveth a perfect picture of it in someone by whom he presupposeth it was done . . . a perfect picture, I say, for he yieldeth to the powers of the mind an image of that whereof the Philosopher bestoweth but a wordish description, which doth neither strike, pierce, nor possess the sight of the soul so much as the other doth.[53]

---

[51] Sidney, op. cit., 610.

[52] Ibid.

[53] Ibid.

Nothing less than a sonnet could adequately sum up Sidney's contribution. So, let me see what I can do.

The Challenge of "The Republic"

Plato banned the poets from his state,

    Yet said, if one could make a sound defense

    In lilting verse, with cogent arguments,

That they do more than merely imitate

An imitation and dissimulate,

    He'd take them back again. And ever since

    Our best minds have been trying to convince

His cautious Guardians of their mistake.

Sir Philip Sidney laid a firm foundation

    In his divine "Defense of Poesy":

The Poet gives us Virtue's exaltation

    More strong than History or Philosophy,

Concretely shows through his imagination

    Not just what is, but more: what ought to be.

Literature according to Sidney then has the serious moral purpose of providing role models that help us to form the ideals and aspirations we live by; it achieves that purpose through concrete images of virtue and vice. Great literature is also fun; as Horace said, it teaches *and* delights. But it does teach. Where in history or experience will you find a better picture of wise counsel than Gandalf, of sacrificial service than Frodo, of loyal friendship than Sam Gamgee, of leadership than Aragorn, of single-minded devotion in love than Aragorn and Arwen, of personal integrity than Faramir? I would hate to have had to live my life without the example and the inspiration that those characters have provided along the way. The point that Peter Jackson apparently does not understand is that Tolkien was not always trying to be realistic in his characters. He is deliberately making up better (and worse) people than we meet in daily life. He is doing it on purpose, for a reason.

Philip, Ronald, and Peter

Hmm. It is no accident that these examples from *The Lord of the Rings* came first and unbidden to my mind. They would have done so even if I had been talking about Sidney outside the context of a chapter on Tolkien. Why? Because Tolkien was very consciously and deliberately following the literary tradition that flows down to us from Sidney through Dr. Johnson and C. S. Lewis. As a result, Tolkien is deliberately giving us characters that strike some moderns—including Peter Jackson—as too good to be true. This is not an artistic flaw; it is central to Tolkien's creative purpose. How shall we enact Faramir's costly integrity in our own lives, for example, if we have never even imagined it to be possible? And how shall we so imagine it if we have never seen it in action? Tolkien's characters perform virtuous deeds that we probably could not perform ourselves—to the end that perhaps someday we can.

Peter Jackson by contrast comes from a more modern tradition that is suspicious of such moral didacticism and is more focused on "realism" (though this realism is somewhat inconsistently pursued, one might think, when it leads to a rabbit-drawn sledge that can travel over dry ground and doesn't need snow, as in Jackson's *The Hobbit*). He apparently thinks the characters Tolkien gave us are too simply good to be fully believable to modern audiences, and so he feels obligated to "complicate" them, to give them internal conflicts other than the ones they actually have, in the hopes that we will better be able to relate to them. Or so his consistent changes to Tolkien's characters would suggest. By this process, Faramir's "I would not take this thing if it lay by the highway"[54] becomes "Tell my father I send him a powerful weapon!" By this process, Aragorn becomes ambivalent about taking up his kingship rather than devoted to his calling with a fixed purpose. By this process, Arwen actually contemplates deserting Aragorn and going to the Grey Havens to escape from Middle Earth despite their earlier pact, and he thinks she would.

By this process of negative moral transformation, in other words, we reach the place where beloved characters are unrecognizable to Tolkien's fans, and they feel betrayed. And they are right to feel so, though mostly they do not understand why. It is because the difference between the books and the movies is not just one of necessary adaptation to a different medium. It is that the author consciously followed the Sidneyan tradition while the adaptor is either ignorant of it or doesn't understand it or has rejected it.

And Tolkien was consciously trying to follow that tradition. He wrote, "I would claim, if I did not think It presumptuous in one so ill-instructed, to have as one object the elucidation of truth, and the encouragement of good morals in this real world, by the ancient device of exemplifying them in unfamiliar embodiments, that may tend to bring them home."[55] His pursuit of that object was, if we may put it in terms, he often used, not wholly in vain.

Now, I am not saying there is no legitimate place in literature for morally conflicted characters; an author can

---

[54] Tolkien, *The Two Towers*, 330.

[55] Tolkien, *Letters*, 194.

profitably show their development toward or away from virtue and portray its consequences—as Tolkien himself did brilliantly with at least one character, Gollum. I am saying that there is a place for the other kind of character Tolkien gave us; that it is an important place; that giving us such characters was in fact what Tolkien was doing; and that Peter Jackson is doing something very different. The difference is not trivial. Jackson cannot imagine unwavering faithfulness, and so gives us an Aragorn who actually thinks about Eowyn and an Arwen who actually thinks about the Havens as real possibilities that can be considered—very unlike the characters in the books.

Tolkien, on the other hand, understood that we need to be able to imagine such things as real virtue and uncompromising integrity. And Tolkien could imagine such things. His guardian, Father Francis, fearing that the young Tolkien's love for his girlfriend, Edith, was distracting him from his schoolwork, had forbidden him to contact her again until he was of age. Tolkien obeyed for three long, hard years; but he also arose from his bed at the very stroke of midnight on his twenty-first birthday to begin a letter to Edith the very second that it was permissible. Thus, he compromised not one whit either his submission to the man he believed was in legitimate authority over him or his devotion to his lady.[56]

Tolkien, in other words, could imagine integrity like Faramir's and a love like Aragorn's and Arwen's because he had lived them himself. He was no doubt enabled to do so by the grace of God, but also partly because his imagination had been fed on literature that many moderns would consider hopelessly naïve, romantic—and didactic.

If you want to be able to live like Tolkien, you had better be able to imagine like Tolkien! Not that you will

---

[56] Humphrey Carpenter, *Tolkien: The Authorized Biography* (Boston: Houghton Mifflin, 1977), 41-3, 60-2.

be able to create imaginary worlds like his, of course; no one has ever done that as well as he did. But you want to be able to feed your mind with the kind of moral imagery writers like Tolkien, Lewis, and George MacDonald themselves fed on and provide in turn for us. They can help you to do that, in ways that Peter Jackson cannot. And Tolkien was able so to help us partly because he had understood and embraced Sir Philip Sidney's profoundly Christian understanding of literature and its purpose.

Oh; and read Sidney, too. For both Tolkien's doing and Sidney's explanation of that doing can strike, pierce, and possess the sight of the soul in ways that few others have ever matched.[57]

Conclusion

Jackson's failure to understand Tolkien's worldview and his philosophy of literature are compounded by sheer Directorial Arrogance. Here we have a book twice independently voted the book of the century, which has for more than fifty years now been loved more intensely by more readers than any other work of fiction ever written. "So, obviously, I, Peter Jackson, have a better idea about what makes a good story and good motivations for the characters than its author did!" It's a good thing the Greek gods don't actually exist. They would surely have noticed the egregious *hubris* (overweening pride) in that assumption by now and be plotting a rather nasty reversal for the career of this, particularly ridiculous mortal.

---

[57] For further discussion of Sidney and the relation of Lewis and Tolkien to his tradition, see Williams, *Inklings of Reality: Essays toward a Christian Philosophy of Letters*, 2nd edition (Lynchburg: Lantern Hollow Press, 2012).

Yet I must admit that, despite all these serious complaints, I was strangely gratified by the movies' popularity and talk of the third being the best picture of the year, even as I was disgusted by the same phenomena for the sake of those who will only see them and not read the books and hence have a false view of many things. For there is an ironic testimony here: Even in such an inexcusably distorted form, much of the power of Tolkien's story still comes through. My favorite comment overheard in the theater was from two theater employees on their way in to clean up after the showing of *The Two Towers*. They had both apparently neither seen the films nor read the books but commented thus: "This must be a movie that makes people think. Everybody always comes out of it very solemn."

And yet . . . and yet . . . they could and *should* have been so much better! All it would have taken was a little more faithfulness, and all that would have taken was a little more trust in Tolkien's work, which might have led to a deeper understanding of its nature and purpose. In an attempt to summarize what went wrong and what was at stake, I can do no better than to offer the following sonnet:

The Quest Motif

(What Lewis and Tolkien Knew,

And Peter Jackson Does Not)

Snaking out across the vast expanse

Of History and Legend lies a trail,

The footing treacherous, the markings pale,

And peril lies in wait for those who chance

To travel it. But if they can advance,

And if their luck and courage do not fail,

They may emerge into a mystic vale

And reach the magic realm of fair Romance.

The landscape's always changing. There is no

Map that can be trusted once you swerve

Aside; your only compass is your quest.

If, true to friend, implacable to foe,

You're faithful to the Vision that you serve,

You'll find that Country which the Muse has
blessed.

One might have hoped, in other words, that Peter Jackson would have had the humility to see himself as the servant of Tolkien's vision. He shows us that, had he done so, he *could* have created a worthy adaptation that would have been a true masterpiece. Instead, he had the arrogance—yea, *hubris*—to make up his own vision and think it better, while outwardly claiming to give us Tolkien's.

Tragic.

INTERLUDE Literary Motifs

Dusk to dusk and dawn to dawn,
Starlight, sunlight slip away.
Ubi Sunt, where have they gone?
All the sages cannot say.

Many things will be restored:
Sanctity in flesh of men;
But hours squandered from the hoard
Never will be seen again.

Ubi Sunt, where have they gone?
All the sages cannot say.
Hence the message of the dawn:
Carpe Diem! Seize the day.

CHAPTER 5 "Lord, Teach Us to Number our Days": The Significance of Tolkien's Elves

The Poet's eye, in a fine frenzy rolling,

Doth glance from heaven to earth, from earth to heaven,

And as imagination bodies forth

The forms of things unknown, the poet's pen

Turns them to shapes, and gives to airy nothing

A local habitation and a name. -- Shakespeare, "A Midsummer Night's Dream"

So, *The Lord of the Rings* treats the symbolism of darkness and light, the strength of dedicated weakness, the value of sacrifice, the hidden government of the world by a purposeful creative providence, and the Christlike nature of true heroism as the powerful biblical truths essential to the very nature, structure, and meaning of the world, that they are. The essay "On Fairie Stories" shows us the Christian worldview at work in Tolkien's understanding of the world. Tolkien's philology enables him to embody that worldview more incarnationally than most writers can ever hope to while illustrating another aspect of the Christian worldview, which begins with "In the beginning was the Word." Peter Jackson's cinematic interpretations of Tolkien's epic show by contrasting with the original the difference Tolkien's Christian worldview made not only to the story he told but to the way in which he told it. What is there left to say? There is one more aspect of Tolkien's Christian vision that still beckons to me like faint torchlight and the barely discernible sounds of revelry glimpsed from afar through the trees of Mirkwood.

TOLKIEN AND THE LORD OF THE RINGS

I have often asked myself what it is that makes *The Lord of the Rings* such a great book. I've asked that question and tried to suggest some answers to it in this writing. It undoubtedly is a great book, arguably the greatest of our time (according to more than one poll), the one people in the next century will be reading when John Grisham and Stephenie Meyer are long forgotten, and even Hemingway and Faulkner read only by English majors. And unless I am badly wrong, they will not only read it but be profoundly moved by it and come to interpret their own lives, as so many of us have done, in terms borrowed from it.

There is, of course, no simple answer to my question. The values the work embodies, the motif of the Quest, the symbol of the Road, the great dramatic conflict of Darkness and Light, the author's absolute mastery of every appropriate style from the homely to the heroic: All these things are no doubt part of the answer. I've tried to show here how its profound reflections of the Christian worldview contribute. But other books have had these elements, if not often all at once or in so much abundance. I suggest that one final ingredient which, acting as a catalyst upon the rest, gives the book its peculiar flavor and enables it to catch our hearts in that grasp that can never be shaken off, is the elves.

Tolkien and the Elves

The elves? What have these pagan, fairy-tale creatures got to do with reality, much less with the Christian worldview? What could be further from a sober biblical view of reality than those airy nothings? Well, wait a moment.

The elves. Frosty starlight on a moonless night. The dancing feet and costly love of Luthien Tinuviel. Cities in the treetops, Caras Galadon, the wind in the leaves of Loth Lorien. Wonder in the eyes of Sam Gamgee. Memories stretching back to days when the world was younger and greener. Wisdom on the brow of Elrond or Galadriel. The last homely house west of the mountains. Ancient blades, wrought with runes, strong for the destruction of evil. Arwen Undomiel, the Evening Star of her people. The fair faces, the grey eyes, the clear voices lifted in song. The songs:

A Elbereth Gilthoniel

Silivren penna miriel

O menel aglar elenath

Na chaired palan-diriel.

O galadhremmin ennorath,

Fanuilos le linnathon

Nef aear, si nef aearon![58]

The Three Rings, unsullied by Sauron. And always, heard as from afar, the sound of the sea.

It is significant that the elves are there. Most men and hobbits have never met one (I have not--at least, not for certain), but we know that they are there in the woods. And the world is a stranger, deeper, brighter place for that knowledge. But far more significant than the fact that they are there is the fact that the elves are leaving. They are exiles, wandering with us for a time, but already they are departing, sailing down Anduin to the sea, to be seen no

---

[58] Tolkien, *Fellowship of the Ring*, op. cit., 296.

93

more. Already our paths are sundered, and the reunion, if there is to be one, is beyond the unmaking of the world.

We know the time is coming--we hope it will not be in our lifetime, but we know it is inevitable and may indeed be already upon us--when the Last Ship will set sail from the Grey Havens, and the work of Cirdan the Shipwright will be at an end. With that ship will sail the last living memory of the Elder Days, and so much more that cannot be named any more than it can be recovered. The woods will be empty, the halls of Rivendell silent. The elves will be gone—lost to us—forever. And that will be that.

It is precisely because the time of the elves is passing away that the beauty associated with them—by implication, all beauty—strikes us so deeply when we walk through the imagined countryside of Middle Earth. They thus become a concrete embodiment of that principle which Shakespeare said should make one's love more strong: "To love that well which thou must leave e're long."[59] Their departing presence is a leaven, kneaded thickly through the whole dough of Tolkien's tale, which gives the loaf that same bittersweet flavor which the strongest joys of the waking world have as their inalienable and unmistakable identifying characteristic.

It is a famous cliche that it is better to have loved and lost than never to have loved at all—none the less true for being a cliche. But it is an even more basic truth that, in this present world, to love *is* to lose. We may love for a long time, and perhaps be faithful even unto death. But the shadow of our mortality lies over everything we see, everything we do, everyone we know. The sunset fades, the symphony ends, the book must be put down, the wife

[59] William Shakespeare, "Sonnet 73," *The Complete Pelican Shakespeare*, ed. Stephen Orgel and A. R. Braunmiller (N.Y.: Penguin, 2002), 85.

or husband dies. Even memories do not last forever. There comes the inevitable parting of paths, the sundering of ways, until, stripped naked, we ourselves fly alone into the Alone.

For it is the simple truth that it is not given to us to possess the beauties of earth. They belong to Another, and we are but allowed to behold them for a moment. We glimpse them out of the corner of our eyes in passing and gaze longingly after them. But we try too hard to hold them, and they slip from our grasp. We stumble into the circle of light, and the torches vanish, the fire goes up in sparks, the revelers and their feast are gone. Then we hear the singing and see the lights again, off yonder through the trees, leading us we know not whither. We only know that we are doomed to seek and never to possess.

This is the burden of Time the Apostle mentioned, under which we walk. Subject to vanity. The bondage of corruption. And beneath it we groan and travail along with the whole cosmos, awaiting our redemption. The words of the Fisherman: all flesh is grass, and all the glory of man is as the flower of grass. The grass withereth, and the flower thereof falleth away (1 Peter 1:24-5); the elves depart from Middle Earth; only the Word of the Lord abides forever.

The elves remind us of the bondage of corruption, this pathos at the heart of all our most moving tales, in at least three ways. The first way is simply through what they are in themselves: embodiments and partakers of a lofty beauty and goodness which we glimpse, and to which some of us aspire, but to which we can never quite attain. It is significant that the two adjectives most frequently used to describe the elves and things elvish are *high* and *fair*. Only a few Elf-Friends like Bilbo or Aragorn dwell at (or even visit) the Last Homely House West of the Mountains, and even their destiny lies elsewhere. And Lorien is a perilous land which few enter and from which fewer return, and none unchanged—essentially because of its strangely alien goodness.

The goodness and beauty of the elves is remote and inaccessible to mortals. It is not something they can attain through effort and attempts to make contact with the elves in that way always come to grief, as the experience of Bilbo and the dwarves in Mirkwood illustrates. When contact is made, as when Frodo is befriended by Gildor Inglorion, it seems on one level to come by chance of luck, but on a deeper level is perceived as having been meant to be; and on the most profound level of all, it is an extension of Grace. And, like the grace of God, it changes our perception of this world by giving us a foretaste, an earnest, of something we will not ever fully have here. It beckons us onward to a land where the longings stirred in us by this beautiful but fallen and temporal world can really be fulfilled. (C. S. Lewis developed this idea of unfulfilled desire as a key to the meaning of life in *Mere Christianity* and in his autobiography, *Surprised by Joy*. Compare Kreeft's fine study of the idea in "C. S. Lewis's Argument from Desire").[60]

The elves remind us of our incompleteness, in the second place, by the fact that even the glimpse of the high and the fair which they offer is being withdrawn. They are themselves exiles in this world, and the longing for Elvenhome across the Western Sea is never quite stilled in them. They, like us, are pilgrims and strangers, but unlike us, they are increasingly anachronisms in what is ever more plainly becoming a world of Men. So they simultaneously remind us of our own essential homelessness and refuse to let us forget the fleetingness of earthly beauty.

---

[60] C. S. Lewis, *Mere Christianity* (N.Y.: MacMillan, 1963), 120; *Surprised by Joy: The Shape of My Early Life* (N.Y.: Harcourt, Brace, and World, 1955); Peter Kreeft, "C. S. Lewis's Argument from Desire," Michael H. MacDonald and Andrew Tadies, eds., *G. K. Chesterton and C. S. Lewis: The Riddle of Joy* (Grand Rapids: Eerdmans, 1989), 249-72.

The ability of the elves to perform these functions for us is intensified by the third thing about them that reminds us of our condition: their immortality within the life of the world. Elves do not die, though they can be killed. Their memories are therefore so long that mere years flit by--a thousand years is as a day. Their experience of time contrasts with ours because of that, which makes the issue of their exile particularly acute for them. For them the years pile up as an ever-increasing burden calling them to rest; for us, our pitifully tiny hoard of years is almost immediately exhausted. For both of us, the years flow swiftly by, the world changes, and the West calls. The elves cannot forget—and hence will not let us forget—the issue of where our real home lies.

All this is a package of meaning that is present whenever an elf is present, reminding us that all beauty is passing and that we ourselves are exiles with no permanent dwelling here, nothing we can keep safe from the ravages of time and the bondage of corruption. The elves keep laying their finger on the heart of that mystery which makes us Man: the ability to glimpse that which keeps us ever wandering, searching on the Road that goes ever on and on. By translating it into a different mode, they make us keep perceiving this fact of our own exile, our search for our true home, the source of that wanderlust which is to us both a sorrow and an incentive to love well what we e'er long must leave. For though we cannot possess beauty, we do love it from afar and see its existence as a message of hope which gives meaning to our very emptiness. And because they do embody beauty, even though it is beyond us and we glimpse it only in passing, the elves are also paradoxically beacons of hope, hope that the goal of our quest exists even if we will never live to see it. They demand, in other words, that we ask ourselves afresh what it means to have received from Iluvatar the gift—or doom—of men.

The Elves and Mankind

For Man does not seem to have been made for the bondage of corruption. The fact that he alone of all creatures feels it *as* a bondage point in that direction. Robert Frost asks pertinently,

> When to the heart of a man
>
> Was it ever less than a treason
>
> To go with the drift of things,
>
> To yield with a grace to reason,
>
> And bow and accept the end
>
> Of love or a season?

This, even though we know in advance that the ending is part of the bargain. So, we continue the search:

> The last lone aster is gone,
>
> The flowers of the witch-hazel wither.
>
> The heart is still aching to seek
>
> But the feet question, "Whither?"[61]

The biblical language speaks of an end to the road for believers in Christ: waiting for the adoption, to wit, the redemption of our body; rebirth, not of corruptible but of incorruptible seed. So, some—Tolkien and his friend C. S. Lewis among them—have thought that we are denied the final fruition of our deepest longings in this life for a reason: that we might be driven to think of the next life and be prepared for union with that Other to whom we also belong.

---

[61] Robert Frost, "Reluctance," *The Poetry of Robert Frost*, ed. Edward Connery Lathem (N. Y.: Holt, Rhinehart and Wilson, 1969), 29-30.

Not that they thought the present life was to be despised or even neglected. It is, after all, the present life, and the future is not yet. It is a necessary place of trial and preparation. It is the arena in which the Quest takes place. It is in it that our redemption will be wrought for us and embraced, here or not at all. Its joys are real joys, its sorrows real sorrows, its good gifts real gifts from above. But it is not All, it is not the End. So with George Herbert, they imagined God bestowing all his good gifts on Man, but withholding one: rest, or satisfaction, or possession.

For if I should (said he)

Bestow this jewell also on my creature,

He would adore my gifts instead of me,

And rest in Nature, not the God of Nature:

So both would losers be.

Yet let him keep the rest,

But keep them with repining restlessness:

Let him be rich and wearie, that at least

If goodnesse leade him not, yet wearinesse

May toss him to my breast.[62]

They asked with Gerard Manley Hopkins if there were anything that could keep back beauty, beauty, beauty from vanishing away, and concluded with him in the negative--but with the hope that elsewhere the things that really matter are kept for us with fonder a care, far with fonder a care than we could have kept them. Where? "Yonder." "What, high as that?" "Yes yonder, yonder. Yonder." And also concluded with him that "We follow,

---

[62] George Herbert, "The Pulley," *The Works of George Herbert*, ed. F. E. Hutchinson (Oxford: Clarendon Press, 1941), 159-60.

now we follow."[63] Beauty was to be loved, as a gift and a signpost, a foretaste and earnest beckoning us onward, but it is not ours to possess--yet. And in the meantime, they would not have disagreed with the atheist Housman that,

> Since to look at things in bloom
>
> Fifty years is little room,
>
> About the woodlands I will go
>
> To see the cherry hung with snow.[64]

The Elves and the Christian Worldview

Not all Tolkien's readers share with this one his hope in the final Eucatastrophe wrought by Christ, the Faerie Tale Hero who was also History and Fact.[65] Which is to say that not all of them have yet responded in faith to the profoundly biblical vision of the world as fallen but redeemed in Christ which permeates every page of his writing. As we have demonstrated here, the biblical vision in Tolkien is ground into the very bones of his imaginary world. But even those who lack an understanding of Tolkien's biblical worldview responds to the bittersweet note of reality sounded so strongly by Tolkien's tale. And it is there precisely because Tolkien's mind was richly imbued with biblical consciousness and hence thought in terms of Creation, Fall, Redemption, Sacrifice, and Grace.[66]

---

[63] Gerard Manley Hopkins, "The Leaden Echo and the Golden Echo," *The Poems of Gerard Manley Hopkins*, ed. W. H. Gardner and N. H. MacKenzie, 4th ed. (London: Oxford Univ. Pr., 1967), 91-3.

[64] A. E. housman, "Loveliest of trees, the cherry now," *The Collected Poems of A. E. Housman* (N. Y.: Holt, Rhinehart and Wilson, 1965), 11.

[65] Tolkien, "On Fairie Stories," op. cit., 71-3.

[66] The best explications of this point are by Kilby, "Mythic and Christian Elements in Tolkien," *Myth, Allegory and Gospel* (Minneapolis: Bethany, 1974), 119-43, and especially in his *Tolkien and the Silmarillion*,

Tolkien's readers live, in other words, in a real-world conditioned by the Fall which begins that even greater Story.

They live in fact in Middle Earth, *middangeard*, in the Old English sense of the word Tolkien borrowed as the name for his imaginary country. For Middle Earth is that middle kingdom, a land which is neither Heaven nor Hell, but borders on both. It is a land of pilgrimage in which there are many goodly inns but no final dwelling place, in which all paths lead inexorably out across those borders which admit of no return. Not all recognize what lies beyond those borders, but all know instinctively that as yet they have found no home. It is undeniable that in this land it is not given to them to possess, and that Tolkien's elves are among the most powerful symbols ever set down of this note of sadness, paradoxically combined with hope, that enters all our tales. As to whether the tale has a happy ending Yonder, those who believe will discover in time. In the meanwhile, Sauron arises again in new and subtle guise; the elves sail down Anduin to the sea; and the Road goes ever on and on.

Near a place where I once lived there is a road, about half a mile in length, which connects two busy thoroughfares but is itself neglected. It was paved with the expectation that houses would grow up beside it, but they were blighted by high interest rates and never sprouted, leaving the scrubby pines to return with impunity. They stand now ten, some fifteen feet high, and have ceased to worry about competition from houses. They are content to provide a haven for squirrels and cover for rabbits and for the moon, which flits from one to another, stalking me over my left shoulder as I walk on those early autumn

---

op. cit., 55ff., where Tolkien himself confirms the basic approach we are taking.

nights that push you out of the house with a restlessness that seems to come from nowhere.

In the middle of the road, invisible from either end, there inexplicably stands a single streetlamp, a monument no doubt to the lunacy of some minor city bureaucrat. It gets electricity from somewhere, somehow, and shines, illuminating only me as I take my solitary journeys. It is an annoying intrusion when you stand beneath its bare rays, but I have not complained to the city fathers, for there is a point on the walk which compensates for all. The leaves of an oak surround the light and shield it, filtering its garish whiteness into a soft green which fades imperceptibly into the blackness of the pines. It is not hard to believe at that moment that you are approaching a convocation of Tolkien's elves, or perhaps the Lantern Waste of Narnia. But, as when one is pursuing the elves of Mirkwood, another step destroys the vision and plunges the walker into a glaring darkness.

That night I knew where the restlessness was coming from, though that knowledge availed me naught in my efforts to evade it. It had flown and caught me from half a world away, where the carefully preserved but very dead body of the president of Egypt lay in state. Normally such news would have elicited only a cynical sigh about the prevalence of evil in the world and little more, but tonight was different. Yet the question which drove my feet toward their rendezvous with the elves was precisely my inability to grieve either for Anwar Sadat or for the world that would have to survive without his rare sanity. For my mind would not focus on that one death but was distracted by the Death that touches all. And that death is embodied concretely for anyone only in the memory of his own most recent dead. Mine was a beagle dog.

I was ashamed of myself for mourning more for a dog months dead than for a man fresh killed, but there it was. She had not even been especially devoted or obedient.

102

But her musical voice had seen me off in the mornings and greeted me coming home. I had shared my sleeping bag with her on nights too cold for any sensible man to be sleeping out of doors. I had held her head in my hands when she groaned in the birth of her puppies. I had watched her front paws drum on the ground in joyous anticipation of supper. And now the physician had told Sadat's wife that "Only Allah is immortal." And his words had struck from half a world away and sent me out to weep beneath a streetlight for the elves which have departed, sailing to the West, returning not.

Conclusion

In this book on the Christian worldview in Tolkien, we have examined the biblical motifs of Creation, Fall, Redemption, Sacrifice, and Grace as they permeate the structure, the plot, the texture, the very flavor of Tolkien's tale. We have spoken of the happy circumstance of having not one but three figures who recall for us different aspects of the life of Christ—Gandalf the prophet, Aragorn the king, Frodo the suffering servant—so that no one character has to shoulder the impossible burden of being the "Christ figure," and all three remain believable while yet together recapitulating the patterns laid down in the life of the Real Redeemer. We have seen how Tolkien can be a doorway to the Christian worldview. We have seen the way that worldview is rooted in the Logos, the Word, as manifest by words. We have seen how attempts to interpret Tolkien's world by people who do not share or understand that worldview falls short of capturing its full richness and majesty.

But time is fleeting, so we will content ourselves now with noticing how Tolkien's elves so wonderfully capture the biblical perspective on the way time is given value by its relation to eternity; with noticing, that is, how his fantasy precisely at its most fantastic is more like the real world than that world can sometimes seem itself. And in noticing that delicious irony, we see not only those tantalizing inklings of reality, not only the rich influence of the Christian worldview on a fertile mind but also the world itself, as it is.

INTERLUDE to Clyde S. Kilby

I

I wandered through the silent trees
Of fair Loth Lorien,
At Cerin-Amroth saw the leaves
Blow o'er the tomb of Arwen.

I wandered North to Rivendell,
To Elrond's homely halls,
And watched as evening shadows fell
On long deserted walls.

Then West I turned, past hill and tree,
'Til I stood by the shore.
But Cirdan was gone, and elves to the sea
Down Anduin sail no more.

II

And I have stood as tall as a king
On a hill top windy and bare
And drunk the air of a Narnian spring
When no one else was there.

And I have seen Cair Paravel
And stood by Aslan's Howe,

But where the king was none could tell
For no one goes there now.

III

And homeward I my feet have turned
But there I never came,
For in my soul a fire burned
And "home" was not the same.

And human eyes I seldom find
Who seem to comprehend
The longing of a pilgrim mind
For distant Fairie lands.

But when I find such eyes, I call
The man who owns them "friend."
And together we wander through leafy halls
In fair Loth Lorien.

CONCLUSION "The Road Goes Ever On": Tolkien and the Quest

In this book, we have looked at how the writings of J. R. R. Tolkien reflect the Christian worldview and how they can help us see what it is and reap the fruits of that vision. We have seen the five biblical motifs—darkness and light, the strength of dedicated weakness, sacrifice, providence, and Christlike heroes—that tie together the plot of *The Lord of the Rings*. We have seen how the essay "On Fairie Stories" shows Tolkien using the Christian worldview that would be incarnated in his fiction to understand the world. We have seen how his philology helped him to practice, in his literary creation, what he preached in the doctrine of sub-creation. We have seen how the application of that Christian worldview to literary composition sets Tolkien's work apart from Peter Jackson's cinematic interpretation of it. And we have seen how his most poignant creation, the elves, drives the beauty of that biblical worldview into our hearts as well as our minds.

So where do we go from here?

I hope my readers will be inspired to read Tolkien more often and enabled to understand him more deeply.

I hope they will be more likely to be helped by that reading of Tolkien in some of the same ways I have been. I hope they will learn to see God in everything so that they need not take off their eyes from anything. I hope they will thus come to be able to find the light that still shines even in their own darkest places. I hope that vision will give them the same hope it gave Sam. I hope they will see it as the light of the glory of God in the face of Jesus Christ.

I hope they will learn from what that light shows them to reckon with their own weakness and to dedicate it rather than despise it. I hope they will come more profoundly to appreciate the great Sacrifice that was made for us all and be enabled to make the sacrifices in its service that are their own lot in life. I hope they will remember that Bilbo was meant to find the Ring and that they will be encouraged by that thought. I hope they will be moved to bow and offer up the hilts of their swords to the great Hero who deserves that service infinitely more even than Tolkien's heroes did, but who deserves it in much the same ways that they did. I hope they will be enabled by all of this to rise to the heroism that their times ask of them. I hope they will step forward to take the Rings that their own lives place in their paths, even though they do not know the way.

I hope they will receive these things, not from me, but from Tolkien. I am just a pointer, saying, "Look! Over there!" I hope they will receive them, not as allegorical meanings imposed on them by the tyranny of the author, but as the "applications" of his work that he made possible for them.[67] These are the applications of Tolkien's work that *I* want them to make, and I think its author would not

---

[67] To understand this hope we must remember Tolkien's own views of "allegory" and "applicability":

> I cordially dislike allegory in all its manifestations, and always have done so since I grew old and wary enough to detect its presence. I much prefer history, true or feigned, with its varied applicability to the thought and experience of readers. I think that many confuse 'applicability' with 'allegory'; but the one resides in the freedom of the reader, and the other in the supposed domination of the author. Tolkien, *The Fellowship of the Ring*, op. cit., 10-11.

An example of an allegorical meaning would be people who thought the Ring a symbol of the atomic bomb. Tolkien assures us that it was not, having been conceived before the bomb was ever heard of. The meaning of the work is not a puzzle to be solved (Ring = Bomb), but if it has been so written as to reflect truth about the world, we will be able to make personal applications of it to our own lives and times without needing to claim that they are what the author was referring to.

be displeased by them. It is clear they are applications of the truth that he made to himself.

The road goes ever on and on. I want my readers to follow it if they can, pursuing it with weary feet until it joins some larger way where many paths and errands meet. They will be well equipped to do so if they have first joined Bilbo, and then Frodo and Sam, on their quests.

And whither then? I cannot say. But I can tell them that Bilbo was meant to find the Ring, and not by its maker. And that may be an encouraging thought.

INTERLUDE Loth Lorien

From silver trunk the golden leaf
Blows through the old abandoned fief,
For Time, the robber and the thief,
Has brought the hidden realm to grief:
The wonder is withdrawn.
Now far beyond the Western Sea
The merry folk have gone to be
Naught but a fading memory
In Caras Galadon.

For untold years Galadriel
Did weave her magic and her spell.
Nor warg nor orc nor dragon fell
Could enter the enchanted veil
Until it was withdrawn.
Now in the once protected Wood
The Evil mingles with the Good—
Foul things that never could have stood
In Caras Galadon.

Now through the hushed and chilling air
There rings no voice of minstrel fair,
No melody of sweetness rare,
No magic words beyond compare;

The music is withdrawn.
The happy sound of harper's glee
Sounds only far beyond the Sea.
The rasping raven's symphony
Fills Caras Galadon.

In Cerin Amroth, Arwen's tomb
Lies hidden in the gathering gloom.
The niphredil no longer bloom.
She sleeps within that narrow room,
All memory withdrawn.
The sons to Aragorn she bore:
They come to mourn her there no more.
They sleep beneath the marble floor
Of cold and deep Rath Dinen, far
From Caras Galadon.

A lonely wanderer passes by;
He sees there is no shelter nigh.
The stars are twinkling in the sky.
He groans, and on the ground doth lie
Within his cloak withdrawn.
The leaves are rustling on high.
It seems to him they softly sigh
A sad lament—he know not why—
In Caras Galadon.

111

APPENDIX Tolkien, Middle Earth, and Narnia: Tolkien's Objections and the Mythical Structure of Narnia

One of the things that people think they know is that Tolkien hated his close friend and fellow Inkling C. S. Lewis's Narnia books, objecting to their allegory, their haste of composition, and their mixing of disparate mythologies, particularly the inappropriate appearances in *The Lion, the Witch, and the Wardrobe* of the faun Tumnus (Roman, pagan) and Father Christmas (Christian). Those who have studied the matter realize that the reality is much more complex—and much more interesting. In this study we will reexamine the question of Tolkien's reaction to Narnia and discover two things: it may not have been what we think, and if it was, it was based on a fundamental misunderstanding of what Lewis was actually attempting.

Tolkien's Reaction

Scholars have long realized that most of what we think we know about Tolkien's reactions to Narnia, including the alleged reasons for it, is based on hearsay. The closest Tolkien ever came to a public statement on the matter was in a letter to David Kolb, S.J., on 11 Nov. 1964: "It is sad that Narnia and all that part of C.S.L.'s work should remain outside the range of my personal sympathy, as much of my work was outside of his."[68] What in Tolkien's work was outside of Lewis's sympathies is hard to say, as Lewis never expressed anything but enthusiastic approval of it. Indeed, as Tolkien admitted more than once, "C. S. Lewis is a very old friend and colleague of mine, and indeed I owe to his encouragement the fact that

---

[68] Tolkien, *Letters*, 352.

in spite of obstacles (including the 1939 war!) I persevered and eventually finished *The Lord of the Rings*."[69] In any case, the note struck by Tolkien's only published reference to Narnia is one more of regret than of the hostility we usually hear about. In fact, Long quotes an unpublished letter from Tolkien to Eileen Elgar dated 24 Dec. 1971:

> I am glad you have discovered Narnia. These stories are deservedly very popular; but since you ask if I like them, the answer is No. I do not like allegory, and least of all religious allegory of this kind. But that is a difference of taste which we both recognized and did not interfere with our friendship.[70]

And his granddaughter Joanna Tolkien reports that Tolkien "handed" her the Narnia books from his bookshelf for her to read.[71] Long comments on the obvious conclusion: "Surely Tolkien thought the Narnia books had some merit."[72] They are according to Tolkien "deservedly" popular and fit reading for his granddaughter—hardly a reaction of unmitigated hostility or hatred.

Nevertheless, the evidence for a much stronger early reaction is not inconsiderable, coming from the testimony of people like Roger Lancelyn Green and George Sayer who knew both Lewis and Tolkien personally.[73] The most substantial passage comes from Sayer:

---

[69] Ibid., 303.

[70] Josh B.Long, Disparaging Narnia: Reconsidering Tolkien's View of Lewis's *The Lion, the Witch, and the Wardrobe*," *Mythlore* 31:3-4 (Spring/Summer 2013): 31-46.

[71] Ibid.

[72] Ibid., 40.

[73] Diana Pavlac Glyer gives a good overview of the situation in *The Company They Keep: C. S. Lewis and J. R. R. Tolkien as Writers in Community* (Kent, Oh.: Kent State Univ. Pr., 2007): 84-6.

The story [*The Lion, the Witch, and the Wardrobe*] was largely finished by the end of the Christmas vacation in 1948. Two months later, Jack read it to Tolkien. Jack had always been constructively helpful and sympathetic with Tolkien's writing, and he probably expected similar treatment. He was hurt, astonished, and discouraged when Tolkien said that he thought the book was almost worthless, that it seemed like a jumble of unrelated mythologies. Because Aslan, the fauns, the White Witch, Father Christmas, the nymphs, and Mr. and Mrs. Beaver had quite distinct mythological or imaginative origins, Tolkien thought that it was a terrible mistake to put them together in Narnia, a single imaginative country. The effect was incongruous, and, for him, painful. But Jack argued that they existed happily together in our minds in real life. Tolkien replied, "Not in mine, or at least not at the same time."[74]

But Sayer never tells us where he got this information. Is it from a conversation he had with Lewis? Did he ever confirm it with Tolkien? We don't know. It may be Sayer's impression of Lewis's impression of Tolkien's reaction—information at third hand, as it were. Still, Roger Lancelyn Green had similar memories and tells us where he got them. He remembered Tolkien once saying to him, "I hear you've been reading Jack's children's story. It really won't do, you know! I mean to say: 'Nymphs and their Ways, The Love Life of a Faun.' Doesn't he know what he's talking about?"[75] The fauns of Roman

---

[74] George Sayer, *Jack: A Life of C. S. Lewis* (Wheaton: Crossway, 1988): 312-13.

[75] Roger Lancelyn Green and Walter Hooper, *C. S. Lewis: A Biography* (N.Y.: Harcourt Brace Jovanovich, 1974): 241.

mythology were infamous for their lechery—hardly fit characters to be friends of Lucy Pevensie!

It is not that we should discount these stories about Tolkien's reaction; they are from sources we have no reason not to trust. But we should remember that what we have above is the extent of the direct data. And it does seem possible that, as it got recycled through various secondary accounts, the story grew in the telling. Hinten, for example, says that "The greatest target of Tolkien's wrath was the appearance of Father Christmas."[76] Yet that information does not appear in any of these memories. Rather, it was Green himself who remembered "reacting against the appearance of Father Christmas . . . and urging Lewis to omit him somehow as breaking the magic for a moment," though Green later came to think that "the rightness of including him seems more certain on each re-reading."[77] That Tolkien included Father Christmas in the list of features of *The Lion, the Witch, and the Wardrobe* to which he objected is probable if we accept Sayer's account, but we do not actually have direct information to the effect that Father Christmas headed that presumed list.

Though its foundations are less firm than we might like, a consensus view of Tolkien's original reaction to Narnia and his reasons for it stems from Humphrey Carpenter's discussion in his early and seminal work *The Inklings*. It is an expansion of his earlier treatment in the Tolkien biography. In *The Inklings*, we learn that Lewis told Green that Tolkien had "disliked [*The Lion, the Witch,*

---

[76] Marvin D. Hinten, "The World of Narnia: Medieval Magic and Morality," *C. S. Lewis: Life, Works, and Legacy*, ed. Bruce L. Edwards, Jr. (London: Praeger, 2007): 72.

[77] Green and Hooper, op. cit., 241.

and the Wardrobe] intensely."[78] Carpenter comments that Tolkien "judges stories . . . by severe standards. He disliked works of the imagination that were written hastily, were inconsistent in their details and were not always convincing in their evocation of a 'secondary world.'"[79] The initial installment of Narnia, *The Lion, the Witch, and the Wardrobe,* offended against all these notions.

> It had been very hastily written, and this haste seemed to suggest that Lewis was not taking the business of 'sub-creation' with what Tolkien regarded as proper seriousness. There were inconsistencies and loose ends in the story, while beyond the immediate demands of the plot the task of making Narnia seem 'real' did not seem to interest Lewis at all. Moreover, the story borrowed so indiscriminately from other mythologies and narratives (fauns, nymphs, Father Christmas, talking animals, anything that seemed useful for the plot) that for Tolkien the suspension of disbelief . . . was simply impossible.[80]

Carpenter does not tell us exactly where he got his information, but Long, probably rightly, says we should not dismiss him because Sayer confirms several elements of his account and Christopher Tolkien vetted the book before it was published.[81]

In summary, we can safely say that Tolkien had an initially negative reaction to *The Lion, the Witch, and the Wardrobe* and never came to like the Narnia books,

---

[78] Humphrey Carpenter, *The Inklings: C. S. Lewis, J. R. R. Tolkien, Charles Williams, and their Friends* (Boston: Houghton Mifflin, 1979): 223.

[79] Ibid., 223.

[80] Ibid., 224.

[81] Long, 36.

though he did come to recognize their value and to recommend them to others in spite of his own inability to appreciate them. He objected to them because of their Christian allegory on his own account, and probably, based on the memories of others, to what seemed to him a hodge-podge of disparate mythologies not truly unified by the careful creation of a believable secondary world with its own mythic and cosmological integrity. That compromise of integrity seemed to him to cut backwards to the mythological sources as well as forward into the new world itself. If you are going to have dwarves, in other words, they should be dwarvish; if you are going to have elves, they should be elvish; and if you are going to have fauns, they should not be left alone with little girls. And (less certainly), you cannot have a Christian figure like Saint Nicholas showing up in a world that has a Lion in place of Christ.

Narnia an Allegory?

What are we to make of these objections? How fair are they? The first thing to notice is that the only one we can trace directly back to Tolkien himself[82] was a mistake. Narnia is not, in fact, a Christian allegory or any kind of allegory at all. It is a story to which Christian symbolism is central, but that is not enough to qualify it as allegory—which raises the question, what is an allegory?

Tolkien never gives a definition. In his essay on Sir Gawain, he contrasts "thinly disguised moral allegory" with the far superior "medium for moral teaching" which is the deep-rooted fairy story.[83] It is well known that in the foreword to the Ballantine edition of his Trilogy he

---

[82] Ibid., 40.

[83] J. R. R. Tolkien, "*Sir Gawain and the Green Knight*," *The Monsters and the Critics and Other Essays*, ed. Christopher Tolkien (London: HarperCollins, 1997): 73.

protested, "I cordially dislike allegory in all its manifestations" and preferred "history, true or feigned" with its "applicability to the thought and experience of the readers." The closest we get to a definition is the idea that allegory comes from the "purposed domination of the author," while application "resides in the freedom of the reader."[84]

Of course, the point at which a suggested symbolic meaning crosses the line into an imposed one would be a bit difficult to chart. And Tolkien's testimony is hard to take with full seriousness in any case. It is difficult to believe that a person who disliked allegory in all its forms and had done so since he could first detect its pernicious presence could have written the allegory of the Tower in the Beowulf essay or the short story "Leaf by Niggle." Rather, we gather that Tolkien disliked forced allegorical interpretations of *The Lord of the Rings*, and wanted to head them off at the pass in no uncertain terms. But that does not help us understand his objection to Narnia.

Lewis strangely never exactly defines allegory either, even in his famous study of it. But there we do learn that in his mind it has to do with the tendency of the human mind to "represent what is immaterial in picturable terms."[85] When that tendency leads to a certain kind of personification, we have allegory.

> You can start with an immaterial fact, such as the passions which you actually experience, and can then create *visibilia* to express them. If you are hesitating between an angry retort and a soft answer, you can express your state of mind by inventing a person called *Ira* with a torch and

---

84 Tolkien, *Fellowship*, 10-11.

85 C. S. Lewis, *The Allegory of Love: A Study in Medieval Tradition* (Oxford: Oxford Univ. Pr. 1958): 44.

3

letting her contend with another invented person called *Patientia*. This is allegory.[86]

There has been a long-running scholarly debate over the accuracy and adequacy of Lewis's concept of allegory since *The Allegory of Love*, and it is beyond the purview of this appendix to go into it. We are interested rather in the notions of allegory that obtained among the Inklings at the time. And there is no evidence that they quibbled with Lewis over that point. Moreover, the Narnia books are not allegories by any definition that does not stretch the term beyond all possibility of usefulness. One standard definition used by literary scholars is that an allegory is

> a form of extended metaphor in which objects, persons, and actions in a narrative . . . are equated with meanings that lie outside the narrative itself. Thus it represents one thing in terms of another—*an abstraction in terms of a concrete image.* . . . It is important that one distinguish allegory from symbolism, which attempts to suggest other levels of meaning without making a structure of ideas a formative influence on the work.[87]

If we do not make that distinction, we render the term allegory meaningless. It would seem that Tolkien failed sufficiently to make it with regard to Narnia, for Aslan symbolizes no abstraction and a whole "structure of ideas" is imposed only in select and isolated scenes such as Aslan's death at the Stone Table.

It is clear then that Lewis did not think of the Narnia books as allegories, and it is easy to see why they are not by the simple expedient of comparing them to his

---

[86] Ibid., 45.

[87] C. Hugh Holman, *A Handbook to Literature*, based on the Original by William Flint Thrall and Addison Hibbard (N.Y.: Bobbs-Merrill, 1972): 13; emphasis added.

actually allegorical book *The Pilgrim's Regress*.[88] Aslan does not represent Christ the way Mother Kirk represents the church or Lady Reason represents reason, or Sigismund represents Freudianism. They are *allegorical* symbols, and Aslan is not. Rather, in Narnia, something else is going on, which Lewis distinguished from allegory by calling it a "supposal." As he explained to a fifth-grade class,

> You are mistaken when you think that everything in the book "represents" something in this world. Things do that in *Pilgrim's Progress*, but I'm not writing in that way. I did not say to myself "Let us represent Jesus as He really is in our world by a Lion in Narnia": I said, "Let us *suppose* that there were a land like Narnia and that the son of God, as He became a Man in our world, became a Lion there, and then imagine what would happen."[89]

Aslan then is not simply a symbol for Christ or a picture of Christ as He actually is in our world, but rather a supposition about what Christ *might* have been like had He been incarnate in a world of talking animals. He is not an allegorical symbol for Christ but a parallel to Christ. Lewis did not think of Narnia as an allegory, but rather as a fairy story—the very genre Tolkien thought was the superior venue for moral instruction. And certainly, Lewis was right about that classification. Lewis explains the effect he was going for:

---

[88] C. S. Lewis, *The Pilgrim's Regress: An Allegorical Apology for Christianity, Reason, and Romanticism* (Grand Rapids: Eerdmans, 1958).

[89] C. S. Lewis, *The Collected Letters of C. S. Lewis*, 3 vols., ed. Walter Hooper (San Francisco: HarperSanFrancisco 2004): 3:479-30, cf. 3:1004; emphasis in the original. For more on Lewis's notion of "supposal" and how it impacts our reading of his fiction, see Williams, *Deeper Magic* 17-18.

I saw how stories of this kind could steal past a certain inhibition which had paralyzed much of my own religion in childhood. Why did one find it so hard to feel as one was told one ought to feel about God or about the sufferings of Christ? I thought that the chief reason was that one was told one ought to. . . . But supposing that by casting all these things into an imaginary world, stripping them of their stained-glass and Sunday school associations, one could make them for the first time appear in their real potency? Could one not thus steal past those watchful dragons?[90]

An allegorical figure *recalls* all the stained-glass and Sunday-school associations; it is not trying to strip them away. Aslan is symbolic of Christ, of course, but he is not that kind of symbol. And Tolkien did not object to symbolism as such. Rather, he would have agreed with Lewis that "The only moral [or doctrinal lesson] that is of any value is that which arises inevitably from the whole cast of the author's mind."[91] And that whole cast of Lewis's mind is precisely the place from which Aslan came bounding into the story.[92]

Tolkien's first objection then seems to have been a genre mistake. If he objected to the Narnia books because they were allegories, he was criticizing them for doing

[90] C. S. Lewis, "Sometimes Fairy Stories May Say Best What's to be Said," *New York Times Book Review, Children's Book Section*, November 1956; rpt. *Of Other Worlds*, ed. Walter Hooper (N.Y.: Harcourt, Brace, Jovanovich, 1964):37.

[91] C. S. Lewis, "On Three Ways of Writing for Children," The Library Association, *Proceedings, Papers, and Summaries of Discussions at the Bournemouth Conference, 29th April to 2nd May 1952*; rpt. *Of Other Worlds*, ed. Walter Hooper (N.Y.: Harcourt, Brace, Jovanovich, 1964): 33.

[92] For more on the Christian meanings in the Narnia books, see Williams, *Mere Humanity* 93-110.

something they were not even trying to do. But if Tolkien had recognized that mistake, it does not follow that he would have changed his mind about the books. There remains a genuine difference in sensibility between him and Lewis that comes into focus here. Tolkien sheds some light on what he might have been trying to say in a comment, not about Narnia but about his own Middle Earth: "Though one may in this [plot elements of *The Lord of the Rings*] be reminded of the Gospels, it is not really the same thing at all. The Incarnation of God is an infinitely greater thing than anything I would dare to write."[93] Well, Lewis had dared to write it! Tolkien reportedly once told Walter Hooper that he thought the Christian elements in *The Chronicles of Narnia* "too obvious."[94] Tolkien did not object to reminders of Christianity as such. He famously said that *The Lord of the Rings* was "a fundamentally religious and Catholic work, unconsciously so at first, but *consciously in the revision*."[95] That is, he deliberately added or strengthened parallels to Christian beliefs in his own story at a certain stage in developing the work. (See chapter one of this book for a study of some of those parallels.) But Hooper's memory rings true, the key phrase being "too obvious." Walsh probably summarizes Tolkien's attitude well: Tolkien

> disapproved of the obvious Christian correspondences. He was attempting a different kind of imaginary world, one overwhelming in its own integrity and relying less on resemblances to the earth and its familiar beliefs. Where Lewis dramatizes the decisive moments of the Christian story, Tolkien slowly, stroke by

---

[93] Tolkien, *Letters*, 237.

[94] Walter Hooper, "Narnia: The Author, the Critics, and the Tale," *The Longing for a Form: Essays on the Fiction of C. S. Lewis*, ed. Peter J. Schackel (Grand Rapids: Baker, 1977): 110.

[95] Tolkien, *Letters*, 172; emphasis added.

stroke, builds up a world that is heroic and tragic.[96]

Both men then wrote religious works, and both wrote them in the same (non-allegorical) manner. But Tolkien had a reticence about doing so overtly and (too) obviously that Lewis did not share. Hooper notes, interestingly, that what had seemed too obvious to Tolkien might not strike others so: "I think this is because he not only knew the Bible better than most of us but also started by knowing what Lewis was 'up to.'"[97] Narnia is not an allegory, but the absence of that reticence allowed Lewis to veer closer to the allegorical, in a scene like the Stone Table, for example, than Tolkien was willing to go. It is not a question of who was right: Many fans of the Inklings are able to appreciate both worlds because they are really just at different points on the spectrum of the same approach. Tolkien was not able to appreciate and did not wish to use, the whole range of that spectrum. His taste was what it was, and he apparently came to recognize its limits himself with some regret before the end. But he obscured the nature of his real objection by calling Narnia an allegory.

A Hodge-Podge of Mythologies?

There is another of Tolkien's apparent issues with the Narnia books that also showed perhaps a bit of uncharacteristic "hastiness" on his part. He reportedly thought that Narnia was not a secondary world with its own mythic integrity but rather a hodge-podge of disparate mythologies, objecting particularly to the appearance of Mr. Tumnus and Father Christmas. Not only did they not belong together in the same world, but

---

[96] Chad Walsh, *The Literary Legacy of C. S. Lewis* (N.Y.: Harcourt Brace Jovanovich, 1979): 155.

[97] Hooper, op.cit., 110.

the faun Tumnus was not even faithful to the well-known nature of fauns.

There are two separate issues here. The first is whether such characters should be in Narnia at all. This would apply to both Tumnus and Father Christmas, as Narnia is neither ancient Rome nor Christian Europe. The second is whether, if they are there, they should be permitted to depart in fundamental ways from their nature as fixed by their mythology of origin. This criticism affects only Tumnus.

There are answers that can be made to both sides of this objection. To the objection to the very presence of such characters, we must say that Tolkien had apparently missed a highly significant fact about the very mythical substructure of Lewis's secondary world. It is not, like Middle Earth, a single, completely self-contained world at all, but is part of what one is almost tempted to call a multiverse. It exists in relationship to other worlds, to all the other worlds in fact that have been created by the Great Emperor over the Sea. And it is full of portals to those worlds: From the Wardrobe in Professor Kirk's spare room to the Painting in the Scrubbs's guest room to the Wood between the Worlds to the Shore of Aslan's Country at the end of the Eastern Sea, Narnia exists—was designed to exist—in relationship to other worlds. And one of those worlds is the England of the protagonist children, which Father Christmas visits annually, and which was once part of ancient Rome.

Many have noted the importance of these portals to the structure of the Narnian universe. McGrath notes that Narnia is connected to "a forest full of entrances to other worlds."[98] Murrin says that the "doors" in Narnia, in general, are "one of the most wonderful things in the

---

[98] Alister McGrath, *C. S. Lewis: A Life* (Carol Stream, Il.: Tyndale House, 2013): 278..

stories."[99]   But so far no one has stressed the relevance of this fact for dealing with Tolkien's objection. What is that relevance?

It would indeed have been inappropriate for such creatures as Tumnus or Father Christmas to show up in Middle Earth. Its history is the prehistory of our world, but its mythology is not any of the mythologies of later peoples, but its own.   The elves and dwarfs of later folklore might be corrupted memories of Tolkien's races, but Eldar are not fairies and Dwarves are not exactly dwarfs. Orcs share only the sound of their name with the *orcneas* of *Beowulf*, and they are not sea monsters but ruined Eldar. Middle Earth shares a timeline with our later world, and it is as insistently linear as that of our own primary world.   There is no mechanism by which later versions of mythological creatures (even if they are later versions of historical races that Tolkien portrays as such) could slip back into the history of Tolkien's Middle Earth without compromising its consistent presentation as history, true or feigned. It would have compromised the integrity of the secondary creation Tolkien was building. Tolkien naturally expected the same kind of creational and artistic integrity from Lewis and did not think he had found it.

But in fact, had Tolkien been able to see it, that integrity was there to be found, at least a greater measure of it than Tolkien was apparently able to perceive. Narnia is not a self-contained world at all but is part of a larger cosmology that not only relates it to Aslan's eternal Country and other temporal worlds but also *connects* it to them via the various kinds of doors and portals that we encounter in almost every story. The full structure of that larger world is not visible at first; it gradually comes into

[99] Michael Murrin, The Multiple Worlds of the Narnia Stories," Word *and Story in C. S. Lewis*, ed. Peter J. Schackel and Charles A. Huttar (Columbia: Univ. of Missouri Pr., 1991): 234.

focus as we move through *The Voyage of the Dawn Treader* and *The Magician's Nephew* to *The Last Battle*. But it is implicit from the very beginning, from Lucy's very first trip through the Wardrobe. Narnia is the kind of world where Father Christmas *could* show up; indeed, given his nature and the nature of the Witch's imposed curse ("always winter and never Christmas"), it is the kind of world in which he could be expected to appear. And given the complicated nature of how Narnian time relates to that of England, there is no reason why Tumnus should not be there either.

There is then a rationale for the appearance of these characters in Narnia that Tolkien was not able to grasp. And once we admit that, we can also discover that their presence was more appropriate (and significant) than he was able to see. Christopher has a good handle on Tolkien's reaction to Tumnus. "Tolkien was bothered as an artist that Lewis's fauns did not obey their own nature," for in Tolkien's mind "they were fixed myths that could be introduced into a secondary world only as the myth had been established."[100] Christopher thinks Tolkien was actually bothered more by the distortion than the mixing of mythologies. "Tolkien is thinking in mythological terms—what is a faun? How can one be expected to act? Lewis is reducing Greek mythology to the pleasant level of a children's story, where the faun is just a picturesque exterior of a nice person."[101] But Lewis did not feel obligated to follow those standards. Gibson has perhaps the best explanation of what Lewis was doing instead. The Narnian doors are more than just mere passageways:

---

[100] Joe Christopher, *C. S. Lewis.* Twayne's English Authors Series. Boston: Twayne, 1987): 118.

[101] Joe Christopher, "J. R. R. Tolkien, Narnian Exile," Mythlore 15:1 (Autumn 1988): 41.

As a creature out of Greek mythology, [Mr. Tumnus] is not a very promising character for a story concerning Christian truth. And that, of course, is the point. Lewis begins with a story, not a theme. From the folklore and fables of many cultures he invites creatures of all sorts— dryads, dragons, giants, and talking animals. And as they enter through the magic portals, the Narnian air works a change in their natures. The Greek centaurs, German dwarfs, British witches, become Narnian through and through. They may be evil or good, but they have the stamp of the new world in which they find themselves.[102]

That Father Christmas plays a significant and non-arbitrary role in the plot has been noted by many. Brown realizes that "From the moment Lewis penned the wonderful line 'always winter and never Christmas,' he had written himself into a literary corner."[103] How is that situation to be reversed without the aid of Father Christmas? Ryken and Meade note that his appearance is not only thematically but structurally significant. "If we regard Father Christmas as part of a symbolic design and as serving an important function of foreshadowing at this midway point of the book, things fall into place" as "the first proof that a great reversal is just around the corner."[104] Indeed. As Gibson notes, "The first indication that, as Mr. Beaver says, 'Aslan is on the move,' is that Father Christmas can no longer be kept out."[105] Even Roger Lancelyn Green, who, as we noted above, initially did not

[102] Evan K. Gibson, *C. S. Lewis, Spinner of Tales: A Guide to his Fiction* (Grand Rapids: Christian College Consortium, 1980): 132.

[103] Devin Brown, *Inside Narnia: A Guide to Exploring* The Lion, the Witch, and the Wardrobe (Grand Rapids: Baker, 2005): 151.

[104] Leland Ryken and Marjorie Lamp Meade, *A Reader's Guide through the Wardrobe: Exploring C. S. Lewis's Classic Story* (Downers Grove: InterVarsity Press, 2005): 75.

[105] Gibson, op. cit., 142.

like Father Christmas's role in Narnia, came to conclude that "the rightness of including him seems more certain on each re-reading."[106] Many readers throughout the decades have resonated with these views. Because the Narnian portals allow for Father Christmas's appearance, we are free to appreciate it for all these reasons, as Tolkien sadly could not.

Conclusion

Tolkien's rejection of Narnia may not have been what many people think. And where he did reject it, those rejections flowed at least partly from misunderstanding, from an inability, in that case, to clearly see what he was looking at. Narnia is not an allegory. It reflected the Christian worldview of its author in much the same way as Middle Earth did that of its author, though in a manner more obvious and overt than that with which Tolkien could be completely comfortable. Narnia is not a mythological hodge-podge. The cosmic structure of its secondary creation makes the appearances of Tumnus and Father Christmas appropriate, just as that of Middle Earth would have made them inappropriate. In later years, Tolkien did not overcome, but came to regret, his inability to enter into Lewis's secondary world. As Long puts it, he "remained indifferent to Narnia, but conceded that there was value in the books for others."[107]

We may be grateful to be those others who have been able to find that value. For many of us, Narnia is a great mythopoeic creation which is the setting for a glorious series of adventures. And for those who share Lewis and Tolkien's faith, it can be something more, as Montgomery explains: "And Narnia—what does Narnia itself symbolize? Narnia is a world, a state of mind, in

---

[106] Green and Hooper, op. cit., 241.

[107] Long, op. cit., 40.

which spiritual issues assume clarity, reality, and a place of paramount importance."[108]

Yes. Value for others, indeed!

---

[108] John Warwick Montgomery, "The Chronicles of Narnia and the Adolescent Reader," Myth, *Allegory, and Gospel: An Interpretation of J. R. R. Tolkien, C. S. Lewis, G. K. Chesterton, and Charles Williams*, ed. John Warwick Montgomery (Minneapolis: Bethany, 1974): 111.

POSTLUDE Some Real Magic

Within the cadences of human speech
Attentive listeners can sometimes hear
The rhythm of the wave upon the beach
Or contemplate the music of the spheres
Within the small sphere of the human eye
The watcher who knows how to look can see
A spirit that's as lofty as the sky
Of humble as the lover on his knee.
When in the alembic of the human mind
Imagination boils with memory,
Such vision with such sound can be combined,
Far more mysterious than alchemy.
The Philosopher's Stone we vainly sought of old
Could never have made such rare and costly
gold.

SELECTED ANNOTATED BIBLIOGRAPHY

Anderson, Douglas A. *The Annotated Hobbit*. Boston: Houghton Mifflin, 2002. Lots of notes.

Bassham, Gregory and Eric Bronson, eds. The Lord of the Rings *and Philosophy*. Chicago: Open Court, 2003. Collection of essays.

Brown, Devin. *The Christian World of* The Hobbit. Nashville: Abingdon, 2012. Spiritual lessons from Middle Earth.

----------. *Inside Narnia: A Guide to Exploring* The Lion, the Witch, and the Wardrobe. Grand Rapids: Baker, 2005. Spiritual lessons from Narnia.

Carpenter, Humphrey. *The Inklings*. Boston: Houghton Mifflin, 1979. Definitive history of Tolkien's circle.

----------. *Tolkien: A Biography*. Boston: Houghton Mifflin, 2007. The standard biography.

Carter, Lin. *Tolkien: A Look Behind* The Lord of the Rings. N.Y.: Ballantine, 1969. Early appreciation.

Christopher, Joe R. *C. S. Lewis*. Twayne's English Authors Series. Boston: Twayne, 1987. Standard reference work on Lewis.

----------. "J. R. R. Tolkien, Narnian Exile." *Mythlore* 15:1 (Autumn 1988):37-45; 15:2 (Winter 1988): 17-23. On Tolkien's reaction to Narnia.

Croft, Janet Brennan. *War and the Works of J. R. R. Tolkien*. London: Praeger, 2004. Influence of WWI on LOTR.

Dickerson, Matthew. *Following Gandalf: Epic Battles and Moral Victory in* The Lord of the Rings. Grand Rapids: Brazos, 2003. Devastating critique of the charge that Tolkien glorifies war.

----------. *A Hobbit's Journey: Discovering the Enchantment of Tolkien's Middle Earth.* Grand Rapids: Brazos, 2012. Expanded version of *Following Gandalf.*

Duriez, Colin. *The J. R. R. Tolkien Handbook: A Comprehensive Guide to His Life, Writings, and World of Middle Earth.* Grand Rapids: Baker, 1991. Glossary of terms, characters, etc. from Tolkien's work.

Ellwood, Gracia Fay. *Good News from Tolkien's Middle Earth.* Grand Rapids: Eerdmans, 1970. On the Christian elements in LOTR.

Flieger, Verlyn. *Splintered Light: Logos and Language in Tolkien's World.* Grand Rapids: Eerdmans, 1983. One of Tolkien's most intelligent and profound interpreters.

Flieger, Verlyn and Douglas Anderson. *Tolkien on Fairy-Stories.* London: HaperCollins, 2008. Commentary on Tolkien's literary theory.

Foster, Robert. *A Guide to Middle Earth.* N.Y.: Ballantine, 1971. A concordance to LOTR.

Frost, Robert. *The Poetry of Robert Frost*, ed. Edward Connery Lathem. N. Y.: Holt, Rhinehart and Wilson, 1969. Source of Frost's poetry quoted here.

Gibson, Evan K. *C. S. Lewis, Spinner of Tales: A Guide to his Fiction.* Grand Rapids: Christian college Consortium, 1980. Literary interpretations of Lewis.

Glyer, Diana Pavlac. *Bandersnatch: C. S. Lewis, J. R. R. Tolkien, and the Creative Collaboration of the Inklings.* Illustr. James A. Owen. Kent, Ohio: Black Squirrel Books, 2016. More popular version of the scholarly *The Company They Keep.*

----------. *The Company they Keep: C. S. Lewis and J. R. R. Tolkien as Writers in Community*. Kent, Oh.: Kent State Univ. Pr., 2007. Updates and corrects Carpenter's *The Inklings*, studying them especially as a writer's group.

Helms, Randall. *Tolkien and the Silmarils*. Boston: Houghton Mifflin, 1981. Early study of *The Silmarillion*.

----------. *Tolkien's World*. Boston: Houghton Mifflin, 1974. Middle Earth in the light of Tolkien's views of fantasy.

Herbert, George. *The Works of George Herbert*, ed. F. E. Hutchinson. Oxford: Clarendon Press, 1941. Standard source of Herbert's poetry.

Green, Roger Lancelyn and Walter Hooper. *C. S. Lewis: A Biography*. N.Y.: Harcourt Brace Jovanovich, 1974. One of the better treatments.

Hillegas, Mark R., ed. *Shadows of Imagination: The Fantasies of C. S. Lewis, J. R. R. Tolkien, and Charles Williams*. Carbondale, IL: Southern Illinois Univ. Pr., 1969. Collection of essays by some of the best Inklings scholars of the mid-Twentieth Century.

Hinten, Marvin D. "The World of Narnia: Medieval Magic and Morality." *C. S. Lewis: Life, Works, and Legacy*, ed. Bruce L. Edwards, Jr. London: Praeger, 2007, 2:71—92. Literary interpretation.

Holman, C. Hugh. *A Handbook to Literature*. Based on the Original by William Flint Thrall and Addison Hibbard. N.Y.: Bobbs-Merrill, 1972. Standard reference work.

Hooper, Walter. "Narnia: The Author, the Critics, and the Tale." *The Longing for a Form: Essays on the Fiction of C. S. Lewis*, ed. Peter J. Schackel. Grand Rapids: Baker, 1977, 105-118. General appreciation.

Hopkins, Gerard Manley. *The Poems of Gerard Manley Hopkins*, ed. W. H. Gardner and N. H. MacKenzie, 4th ed. London: Oxford Univ. Pr., 1967. Standard source.

Housman, A. E. *The Collected Poems of A. E. Housman.* N. Y.: Holt, Rhinehart and Wilson, 1965. Standard source.

Isaacs, Neil D. and Rose A. Zimbardo. *Tolkien and the Critics: Essays on J. R. R. Tolkien's* The Lord of the Rings. Notre Dame: Univ. of Notre Dame Pr., 1968. Earlier version of Zimbardo & Isaacs contains several essays not in the later collection.

Kilby, Clyde S. *Tolkien and* The Silmarillion: *A Glimpse of the Man and his World.* Wheaton: Harold Shaw, 1976. Early and insightful glimpse at *The Silmarillion* by the dean of American Inklings scholars and founder of the Wade Collection at Wheaton College, Illinois. Kilby spent a summer helping Tolkien get his notes for the book in order.

-----------. "Mythic and Christian Elements in Tolkien." *Myth, Allegory, and Gospel: An Interpretation of J. R. R. Tolkien, C. S. Lewis, G. K. Chesterton, and Charles Williams.* Ed. John Warwick Montgomery. Minneapolis: Bethany Fellowship, 1974, 119-43. Excellent early treatment.

Kocher, Paul H. *Master of Middle Earth: The Fiction of J. R. R. Tolkien.* Boston: Houghton Mifflin, 1972. One of the first works to take account of the short fiction in relation to the Middle Earth saga.

Kreeft, Peter J. "C. S. Lewis's Argument from Desire." Michael H. MacDonald and Andrew Tadies, eds., *G. K. Chesterton and C. S. Lewis: The Riddle of Joy.* Grand Rapids: Eerdmans, 1989, 249-72. Analysis of Lewis's apologetic use of longing, relevant perhaps to the Elves' longing for the sea in Middle Earth.

----------. *The Philosophy of Tolkien: The Worldview behind* The Lord of the Rings. San Francisco: Ignatius, 2005. Asks a series of philosophical questions and gives answers with reference to Tolkien's works.

Lewis, C. S. *The Allegory of Love: A Study in Medieval Tradition.* Oxford: Oxford Univ. Pr. 1958. Lewis on allegory.

----------. *The Collected Letters of C. S. Lewis*, 3 vols., ed. Walter Hooper. San Francisco: HarperSanFrancisco 2004. Indispensable source on Lewis's life and thought.

----------. *The Last Battle.* 1956; N.Y.: HarperCollins, 1994. The conclusion to the Narnia books.

----------. *The Lion, the Witch, and the Wardrobe.* 1950; N.Y.: HarperCollins, 1994. Introduction to Narnia.

----------. *Mere Christianity.* N.Y.: MacMillan, 1943. Lewis's exposition of the Christian world view.

----------. "On Three Ways of Writing for Children." The Library Association. *Proceedings, Papers, and Summaries of Discussions at the Bournemouth Conference, 29th April to 2nd May 1952*; rpt. *Of Other Worlds*, ed. Walter Hooper. N.Y.: Harcourt, Brace, Jovanovich, 1964: 22-34. Lewis on writing children's books.

----------. *The Pilgrim's Regress: An Allegorical Apology for Christianity, Reason, and Romanticism.* Grand Rapids: Eerdmans, 1958. Early allegorical work by Lewis.

----------. "Sometimes Fairy Stories May Say Best What's to be Said." *New York Times Book Review, Children's Book Section*, November 1956; rpt. *Of Other Worlds*, ed. Walter Hooper. N.Y.: Harcourt, Brace,

Jovanovich, 1964:35-38. Essay on fairy stories; cf. Tolkien's essay on that topic.

----------. *Surprised by Joy: The Shape of my Early Life*. N.Y.: Harcourt, Brace, and World, 1955. Lewis's spiritual autobiography.

----------. *The Voyage of the Dawn Treader*. 1952; N.Y.: HarperCollins, 1994. Introduces us to Aslan's Country.

Lobdell, Jared. *England and Always: Tolkien's World of the Rings*. Grand Rapids: Eerdmans, 1981. The Ring trilogy as a new mythology for England.

----------, ed. *A Tolkien Compass*. Chicago: Open Court, 2003. Collection of essays.

Long, Josh B. Disparaging Narnia: Reconsidering Tolkien's View of Lewis's *The Lion, the Witch, and the Wardrobe*." *Mythlore* 31:3-4 (Spring/Summer 2013): 31-46. Excellent source on Tolkien's evolving view of Narnia.

Markos, Louis. *On the Shoulders of Hobbits: The Road to Virtue with Tolkien and Lewis*. Chicago: Moody, 2012. Spiritual lessons from Narnia and Middle Earth.

McGrath, Alister. *C. S. Lewis: A Life*. Carol Stream, Il.: Tyndale House, 2013. Recent biography of Lewis has rigorous review of sources.

Mills, David. "The Writer of our Story: Divine Providence in *The Lord of the Rings*." *Touchstone: A Journal of Mere Christianity* 15 (2002), 22-28. Christian interpretation.

Montgomery, John Warwick, ed. *Myth, Allegory, and Gospel: An Interpretation of J. R. R. Tolkien, C. S. Lewis, G. K. Chesterton, and Charles Williams*. Minneapolis: Bethany, 1974. Includes seminal essay by Kilby on "Mythic and Christian Elements in Tolkien" and by Montgomery on Narnia and the adolescent reader.

Morison, Frank. *Who Moved the Stone?* Downers Grove, Il.: InterVarsity Press, n.d. Classic defense of the historicity of the resurrection of Christ.

Moseley, Charles. *J. R. R. Tolkien.* Plymouth, England: Northcote House, 1997. British biography with good spiritual insight.

Murrin, Michael. "The Multiple Worlds of the Narnia Stories." *Word and Story in C. S. Lewis,* ed. Peter J. Schackel and Charles A. Huttar. Columbia: Univ. of Missouri Pr., 1991, 232-55. On Narnian cosmology and portals.

Noel, Ruth S. *The Languages of Tolkien's Middle Earth.* Boston: Houghton Mifflin, 1974. Good place to start for linguistics.

Pfotenhauer, Paul. "Christian Themes in Tolkien." *Cresset* 32 (January 1969), 13-15. Early treatment.

Pearce, Joseph. Tolkien: *Man and Myth.* New York: HarperCollins, 1999. Spiritual biography.

Purtill, Richard L. *J. R. R. Tolkien: Myth, Morality, and Religion.* San Francisco: Harper and Row, 1985. Good general treatment.

----------. *Lord of Elves and Eldils: Fantasy and Philosophy in C. S. Lewis and J. R. R. Tolkien.* Grand Rapids: Zondervan, 1974. Title is self-explanatory.

Reilly, R. J. *Romantic Religion: A Study of Barfield, Lewis, Williams, and Tolkien.* Athens: Univ. of Georgia Press, 1971. Tries perhaps a bit too hard to see Barfield as the key to the Inklings' work.

Reynolds, Patricia and Glen H. Goodknight, eds., *Proceedings of the J. R. R. Tolkien Centenary Conference, Keble College, Oxford, 1992.* Altadena, CA: The Mythopoeic Pr., 1995. Substantial collection of essays.

Roby, Kinley E. *J. R. R. Tolkien.* Twayne's English Authors Series. Boston: G. K. Hall, 1980. Basic biographical information.

Rutledge, Fleming H. *The Battle for Middle Earth: Tolkien's Divine Design in The Lord of the Rings.* Grand Rapids: Eerdmans, 2004. Christian interpretation.

Ryken, Leland and Marjorie Lamp Mead. *A Reader's Guide through the Wardrobe: Exploring C. S. Lewis's Classic Story.* Downers Grove: InterVarsity Press, 2005. Literary value and spiritual meaning.

Salu, Mary and Robert T. Farrell, eds. *J. R. R. Tolkien, Scholar and Storyteller: Essays in Memoriam.* Ithaca: Cornell Univ. Pr., 1979. Substantial collection of essays.

Sayer, George. *Jack: A Life of C. S. Lewis.* Wheaton: Crossway, 1988. Many consider it to be the best life of Lewis overall.

Schaeffer, Francis. *The God Who is There: Speaking Historic Christianity into the Twentieth Century.* Downers Grove, Il.: InterVarsity Press, 1968. Introduction to the Christian world view.

----------. *He is There and He is Not Silent.* Wheaton: Tyndale House, 1972. How the Christian world view has better answers to the basic philosophical questions.

Scull, Christina, and Wayne G. Hammond. *The J. R. R. Tolkien Companion and Guide*, 2 vols. Boston: Houghton Mifflin, 2006. Massive and magisterial reference work.

Shakespeare, William. *The Complete Pelican Shakespeare*, ed. Stephen Orgel and A. R. Braunmuller. N. Y.: Pelican, 2002. Basic source.

Shippey, T. A. "Creation from Philology in *The Lord of the Rings*." in Salu, Mary and Robert T. Farrell, eds. *J.*

R. R. Tolkien, Scholar and Storyteller: Essays in Memoriam. Ithaca: Cornell Univ. Pr., 1979: 286-316. Superb essay on the role of language creation in the creation of Middle Earth.

----------. *J. R. R. Tolkien: Author of the Century.* Boston: Houghton Mifflin, 2002. Newer work by the dean of Tolkien scholars.

----------. *The Road to Middle Earth: How J. R. R. Tolkien Created a new Mythology.* London: Grafton, 1982. Most important single work of Tolkien scholarship, by Tolkien's successor as professor of Anglo-Saxon at Oxford.

Tolkien, J. R. R. *The Fellowship of the Ring.* New York: Ballantine Books, 1982. First volume of the trilogy.

----------. *The Hobbit.* New York: Ballantine Books, 1982. The book that started it all.

----------. "Leaf by Niggle." *The Tolkien Reader.* N.Y.: Ballantine, 1966: 85-112. Allegorical and autobiographical short story.

----------. *The Letters of J. R. R. Tolkien.* Selected and edited by Humphrey Carpenter, with the assistance of Christopher Tolkien. Boston: Houghton Mifflin, 1981. Important source for Tolkien's own views.

----------. "On Faerie Stories." *The Tolkien Reader.* NY: Ballantine, 1966, pp. 3-84. Seminal essay; source of the doctrine of sub-creation.

----------. *The Return of the King.* New York: Ballantine Books, 1982. Final installment of the trilogy.

----------. *The Silmarillion.* Boston: Houghton Mifflin Co., 1977. Prequel to the trilogy.

----------. "*Sir Gawain and the Green Knight.*" *The Monsters and the Critics and Other Essays*, ed. Christopher

139

Tolkien. London: HarperCollins, 1997: 72-108. Insights on Tolkien's view of allegory.

----------. *The Two Towers*. New York: Ballantine Books, 1982. Middle book in the trilogy.

Urang, Gunnar. *Shadows of Heaven: Religion and Fantasy in the Writings of C. S. Lewis, Charles Williams, and J. R. R. Tolkien*. Philadelphia: Pilgrim Press, 1971. Early attempt to critique both the fiction and the ideas it embodies, vitiated by its modernist perspective.

Walsh, Chad. *The Literary Legacy of C. S. Lewis*. N.Y.: Harcourt Brace Jovanovich, 1979. Literary interpretation.

Williams, Donald T. *Deeper Magic: The Theology behind the Writings of C. S. Lewis*. Baltimore: Square Halo Books, 2016. Does for Lewis what this book does for Tolkien, in greater detail.

----------. *Inklings of Reality: Essays toward a Christian Philosophy of Letters*. Toccoa Falls, GA: Toccoa Falls College Press, 1996; 2nd ed., revised and expanded, Lynchburg: Lantern Hollow Press, 2012. Tolkien makes a significant appearance in chapters 1 and 2; chapter 8 (in the 2nd ed., chapter 11) is devoted to him. More detail on the philosophy of reading I have tried to encourage here.

----------. "'Is Man a Myth?': Mere Christian Perspectives on the Human," *Mythlore* 23:1 (Summer/fall 2000): 4-19. Chesterton, Lewis, and Tolkien on human nature; was expanded later into the book *Mere Humanity*.

----------. "Lord, Teach Us to Number our Days: The Significance of Tolkien's Elves." *Inklings of Reality: Essays toward a Christian Philosophy of Letters*, 2nd ed. Lynchburg: Lantern Hollow Press, 2012: 217-228. Tolkien's version of *sensucht* as a key to the meaning of the Ring trilogy; adapted as a chapter here.

----------. *Mere Humanity: Christian Perspectives on the Human from G. K. Chesterton, C. S. Lewis, and J. R. R. Tolkien.* Nashville: Broadman & Holman, 2006. Expansion of "Is Man a Myth?" (q.v.); Tolkien *et al.* as antidotes to secularist reductionism. Interprets Tolkien's fiction in the light of his view of human nature and purpose in "On Fairie Stories."

----------. Review of Mark Eddy Smith, *Tolkien's Ordinary Virtues: Exploring the Spiritual Themes of* The Lord of the Rings (Intervarsity, 2002) and Matthew Dickerson, *Following Gandalf: Epic Battles and Moral Victory in* The Lord of the Rings (Brazos, 2003), in *Trinity Journal* NS 26:2 (Fall 2005): 352-3. Review of a mediocre book on Tolkien (Smith), and a good one (Dickerson).

----------. Review of Peter Jackson's "Return of the King," *Mythprint: The Monthly Bulletin of the Mythopoeic Society* 41:1 (Jan. 2004): 12-13. Failure of Jackson's movies accurately to reflect Tolkien's vision; expanded to become chapter four of this book.

----------. *Stars through the Clouds: The Collected Poetry of Donald T. Williams.* Lynchburg: Lantern Hollow Press, 2011. Source of the author's poems in this book.

----------. "An Unexpected Meeting" (short story), *The Lamp-Post* 29:1 (Spring 2005, published Spring 2007), 3-7. Lewis and Tolkien come back to check up on Inklings II.

----------. "The World of the Rings: Why Peter Jackson Was Unable to Film Tolkien's Moral Tale," *Touchstone: A Journal of Mere Christianity* 26:6 (Nov.-Dec. 2013): 14-16. Some of the changes Jackson made to the books explained by divergent views of the nature and purpose of literature. Expanded to become chapter 4 of this book.

Witherspoon, Alexander M. and Frank J. Warnke. *Seventeenth-Century Prose and Poetry*, 2nd ed. N.Y.:

Harcourt Brace Jovanovich, 1982. Source of quotations from Donne.

Wood, Ralph C. *The Gospel According to Tolkien: Visions of the Kingdom in Middle Earth*. Louisville: Westminster John Knox Press, 2003. Good on Tolkien's eschatology (see chp. 5).

Zimbardo, Rose A. and Neil D. Isaacs. *Understanding The Lord of the Rings: The Best of Tolkien Criticism*. Boston: Houghton Mifflin, 2004. Best collection of essays.

A FINAL WORD

TO J. R. R. TOLKIEN

On a day when Fall's first leaves were flying
And the wind was howling and geese were crying
And clouds were black and the sun was hiding,
Word first came, on dark wings riding.

"Tolkien is dead,"
Was all they said,
And left us crying.

He heard by light of star and moon
The Elven songs and learned their tunes.
He had long walks with them, and talks,
Beneath the swaying trees in June.

Dwarf-mines deeply delved he saw
Where Mithril glittered on the walls
And mighty kings wrought wondrous things
And reigned in hollow, torch-lit halls.

To forests wild and deep he went

And many lives of men he spent
Where leaves of years fall soft like tears,
Listening to the speech of Ents.

In lofty halls of men he sat
Or rustic rooms of bar-man fat;
In hobbit holes, heard stories told
By an old man in a wizard's hat.

With magic words of dark and light
And days of doom and coming night
And magic rings and hoped for spring,
He wrought the record of his sight. . . .

In Beowulf's bold fleet he sailed,
With Gawain the Green Knight beheld;
By Beortnoth's side he stood and cried
As hordes of pagan Danes he felled,

"Will shall be sterner, heart the bolder,
Spirit the greater as our strength fails!'

On a day when Fall's first leaves were flying
And the wind was howling and geese were crying
And clouds were black and the sun was hiding,

Word first came, on dark wings riding.

"Tolkien is dead,"
Was all they said,
And left us crying.

GENERAL INDEX

149

www.ingramcontent.com/pod-product-compliance
Lightning Source LLC
La Vergne TN
LVHW051739080426
835511LV00018B/3143